actually, it's **love**

True love stories of the rich and famous

actually, it's **love**

John McGowan and Frankie McGowan

BLAKE

Published by Blake Publishing Ltd,
3, Bramber Court, 2 Bramber Road,
London W14 9PB, England

www.blake.co.uk

First published in paperback in 2004

ISBN 1 85782 532 2

British Library Cataloguing-in-Publication Data:

A catalogue record for this book is available from the British Library.

Design by www.envydesign.co.uk

Printed in Great Britain by Bookmarque, Croydon

1 3 5 7 9 10 8 6 4 2

Papers used by Blake Publishing are natural, recyclable products made from
wood grown in sustainable forests. The manufacturing processes conform to the
environmental regulations of the country of origin.

Contents

Foreword

OVER THE YEARS, literally thousands of wonderful people up and down the land and from all walks of life have helped raise money for ROC (Research into Ovarian Cancer) by running, swimming, dancing, cycling, selling cakes, holding raffles and discos, giving concerts and doing the hundred and one other incredible, ingenious, amusing things that fundraisers come up with. Publishing this book is another of those things.

And why? Because each year over 5,500 women in the UK contract ovarian cancer, and 4,500 die from it. In 1992, ROC was established following the deaths of two of those women – my wife Angela McGowan and Pamela Cullen, mother of founder member John (JC) Cullen. The intention was to fund research into the development of a blood test which, together with ultrasound scanning, could detect the disease in its primary stage. Ovarian cancer is known as 'The Silent Killer' because it has few obvious symptoms to alert someone to its development. Yet, if it can be caught early enough then it is treatable in well over ninety per cent of cases.

Recently, grants from organisations including the Medical Research Council have meant that the research project ROC has been supporting has benefited by over £23 million. It is anticipated that, after a huge screening operation has been completed, a simple blood test will be available through the National Health Service which will detect ovarian cancer in its infancy.

So, job done? Not a bit of it. ROC is now turning its attention from detection to prevention. The next stage of its effort will be to support projects studying the causes of the development of ovarian cancer.

Everyone involved in the compilation of this book is therefore delighted and very grateful indeed to all the wonderfully generous people who have given their invaluable time and talent to contribute their story, including our highly valued patron Michael Ball who has, with Cathy, also organised so many star-studded fundraising concerts for ROC.

I would also like to extend warm and appreciative thanks to our terrific publisher John Blake who has once again so generously supported ROC. Extra special thanks to Rosie Ries who has been hugely supportive throughout, and also many thanks to Michelle Signore, Skye Wheeler, Adam Parfitt and Graeme Andrew without whom … Many thanks also go to Peter Glossop who figured out the technical stuff in the preparation of this book; and the endless list of people – they know who they are – who helped get so many people to meet deadlines;

and, as ever, a big thank you to Amy Glossop who also helped put so much in place.

Finally, if you would like to know more about ROC or wish to help through a donation, we would really like to hear from you. You can reach us at:

ROC
PO Box 3872
London SW15 1XR
Tel: 020 8798 1406
Fax: 020 8798 1008
Email: penelopefhobbs@roc-charity.org
Website: www.roc-charity.org

However, just by buying this book you have already made a valuable difference to the work of ROC. Thank you.

John McGowan
Chairman

MICHAEL BALL

Michael Ball, the number-one award-winning musical star in the UK, has starred in Phantom Of The Opera, Les Miserables *and, both in London and on Broadway, in* Aspects of Love. *Most recently he starred in* Chitty Chitty Bang Bang. *He has also recorded eleven gold and platinum solo albums. Michael is the patron of ROC which he helped set up and for which he is a tireless fundraiser.*

actually, it's **love**

Then There Was The Time

Romantic love is pretty wonderful, no question. And it can certainly turn your life upside down. But it isn't the only kind of love in the world that hits hard. There's another kind: the one that takes your life by the scruff of the neck, demolishes rational thinking and casts aside any sensible person's grip on reality. For me it's what I do for a living. From the moment when, aged ten, I was taken to see *Jesus Christ Superstar*, the die was cast.

It wasn't always like that. If only. In my time, and in the pursuit of romantic love, I'm surprised the phrase 'slightly unhinged' wasn't permanently applied to me. There was, after all, plenty of evidence to prove it.

At the sort of age when blokes think the height of literary genius is on the lines of 'roses are red, violets are blue, you're a right raver, I'm stuck on you' (ah c'mon, I was only fourteen), my grip on common sense was coloured by the need for instant results, not a prize for literature. Now if at fourteen I'd been up to something a bit more soulful such as 'Shall I compare thee to a summer's day?' rather than sounding like a fully paid-up member of Ozzie Osbourne's fan club, the object of my affections might have put me up on the same pedestal as she put Bruce Springsteen; instead I was reduced to watching her swan off with a much older bloke – with a car – leaving me to stick on my bedroom wall a bitter little note that said: 'Romance: see under "****"'.

God knows where the card is now. Long gone, I suppose, leaving only the dimmest recollection of what the fuss was all about, and replaced by a slightly firmer grip on reality and the unexpected discovery that romantic love – wonderful though it is – doesn't have the field to itself. This other, different but equally powerful love is the force that underpins the way I live; without it, I couldn't work.

Only love, you see, could get me on that stage, into the recording studios, through the interviews, on the tours, riding out the setbacks and punching the air with delight when they've been overcome. And, believe me, there have been some tricky moments that no one ever sees when I'm on stage, when it looked as though I was going to come unstuck just getting there.

Got a minute? OK, pour a glass of wine, put your feet up and let me tell you what can happen in the name of love.

There have been plenty of times when I've staggered on stage with a temperature pushing through the roof, a couple of times when I've left music scores in the backs of cabs and spent frantic hours trying to retrieve them, and more than once the song 'Singing In The Rain' has taken on a whole new dimension at open-air concerts and the words 'rats' and 'drowned' appeared in the same sentence.

Then there was the time when London was gridlocked in the grip of a heatwave and the car sent to collect me couldn't even get past the corner of the road where I live. So what would any sane person do? Get on a bike. A fold-up one in the boot, used for gentle cycles round the nearest park or meandering along a deserted beach, was unceremoniously dragged out and, with a group of slack-jawed bystanders watching, I pedalled out into the traffic. I know now why cyclists hate motorists, but that's another story.

After weaving in and out of cars, lorries and buses, squeezing through gaps the size of a pencil in the seized-up mass of rush-hour traffic, I reached Her Majesty's Theatre in Haymarket with less than a minute to spare. All I'm saying is I lost enough weight in exertion and sweat to make my stage suit feel a little loose that night, and make-up couldn't totally disguise the scarlet face.

I should gloss over the small matter of being asked to open *Chitty Chitty Bang Bang* at the Palladium, playing Caractacus Potts, but what the hell. The ink was dry on the contract before it occurred to me that maybe I should tell someone I'd never had a dancing lesson in my life. Like everyone else, I saw the movie when I was a kid and loved it. I knew the show was for me. Not that I have a mechanical bone in my body – in fact I'm to car maintenance what Lily Savage is to sobriety. But this musical had the whole package: energy, brilliant songs and a great story. I was going to get to dance, to act, to sing and to work with the best in the business. So what if I didn't know a Tango from a Time Step? How hard could that be?

But anyone watching on the sidelines as I embarked on a crash course in dancing under the tutelage of the legendary, brilliant choreographer Gillian Lynne would be forgiven for thinking my tenuous grip on sanity might have snapped. I would go home at night after rehearsals and be aware of muscles in my body I never knew existed. But slowly – crushingly slowly in my case – it began to feel less like a training session with a crazed Sumo wrestler as the faint possibility dawned on me that I might actually walk out of rehearsals without clutching the walls for support. When I finally did, I'm amazed everyone didn't shriek, 'By Jove! I think he's got it!'

And then there was Manhattan last summer. The album I had gone there to finish – with a final duet with my mate Antonio Banderas – came this close to being scuppered when the whole town was plunged into darkness in the biggest power failure in the history of the

US. You might think there are worse places to be stuck in a blackout, and you would be right.

But, after a night when the entire city had been reduced to an eerie but extraordinary and exhilarating street party, the lights came on. Almost everywhere. Just not on the street where the Hit Factory is located and where we were due to record. I just put my head in my hands. Antonio had to be back on stage that evening, and I had to be on a plane to London. All we could do was hit the phones and call up everyone and anyone who might be able to help.

With the clock ticking and the situation looking hopeless, a call suddenly came from Sony across town who had just had their power restored. They had a small window in their schedule if Antonio and I could get there. There was no question of a cab – abandoned cars from the night before were still blocking every street and the subway was still out. It was just a case of 'last one there buys the drinks' and off we sprinted. Antonio won, but that's only – and never mind what he says – because he knew the way.

With only minutes to spare, and cheered on by Julio Iglesias who had swung by to see us, we had recorded 'Me And My Shadow' and the album was complete. The track was in the bag, Antonio made it back on stage and I legged it for the airport.

And the title of the album? *A Love Story*. What else?

ULRIKA JONSSON

Ulrika Jonsson shot to fame hosting Gladiators. *She has since appeared in numerous shows including* Shooting Stars, *and won praise for her interviews with leading politicians for* The Great Big Election Programme *and* Ulrika in Euroland. *Her autobiography* Honest *was published in 2002 and became an instant bestseller.*

actually, it's **love**

The Truth About Love

Dear God

If it is true that you are love, tell me what is it that makes my heart swell when I look at the fingers of my newborn?

What is it I feel in my stomach like a thousand butterflies desperate to escape when my husband throws me a glance across the room?

What is it that makes my eyes fill with tears when I see the blind man on the bus and the small child with no shoes on her feet?

That, too, is surely love.

I know love. I know I love my parents, but I can feel the love I have for my children. I acknowledge the love my husband sends me. But it is my purpose to give good love. I have found it hard to receive love, for to receive it is much more difficult than to give. I haven't cared enough about the love of myself, I have abandoned it, in lieu of the gift of giving.

When I feel love, it makes me cry and it makes me weak. It reduces my defences, but still I love to love. I accept the love my children give without question. All other loves are interrogated. But I know love can make me strong, and without it I will be truly nothing.

So I will accept receipt of the love of my husband with all the grace of a character in *Pride and Prejudice*. But I will go on loving the stranger on the bus and the child with no shoes and no name. For I, too, am love. And not God alone.

SIR IAN McKELLEN

Sir Ian McKellen is internationally renowned as the leading British actor of his generation. His performances in Shakespeare and other classics on stage and screen are legendary. With over forty acting awards to his name, he has most recently earned acclaim as Gandalf in the Oscar-winning trilogy The Lord of The Rings.

actually, it's **love**

Love's Labours Won

In the autumn of 1987, I returned to London after a year working hard in the USA. I had been touring hither and thither in my solo show, *Acting Shakespeare*, and had earned enough dollars to take a sustained holiday. My plan was to stay at home, find my friends again and take time out to try and understand what I wanted to work on next. I even had doubts as to whether I wanted to carry on acting.

At a lunch party, I met up with a friend who, in my absence, had transformed himself. When I went to America, he had been a fast-living businessman, a restless achiever. Now he was calm, obviously at ease with his new life. He had given up his share of the business and was working, almost full time, as a volunteer for London Lighthouse. He was radiant as he described the new centre devoted to people with HIV and AIDS which helped them and their families to cope with their desperately changed circumstances.

An abandoned school in Notting Hill Gate was being

rebuilt to provide meeting rooms for counselling, with a café and garden at the back and a residential floor on top with twenty-six beds where the sick could recuperate and the dying rest in peace.

What a vision. And what a transformation it had inspired in my friend.

The building was being financed in part by a government grant – after all, some might mistakenly think the volunteers were doing the work of the National Health Service. But when I heard about it all, disaster was imminent. The public money was late in arriving and Christopher Spence, the director of London Lighthouse, was about to send the builders home with no certainty that he would ever be able to afford to get them back.

So that's how I came to do *Acting Shakespeare* for ten weeks at the Playhouse in London's West End. I've never known a show organised with so little trouble. The idea was simple. We would tell the audiences that every penny (minus VAT) would go to the Lighthouse, where their donations would be transformed overnight into bricks and mortar for one of the most imaginative new buildings in London. The Playhouse scarcely charged us rent, even though it was agreed that their staff should be paid. A philanthropist underwrote the inevitable costs of publicity.

After each performance, I bullied my willing audiences to fill the red buckets, which I and other Lighthouse volunteers held out in the theatre foyer. Over the three months, we raised about £500,000. No sooner was that achieved than the government's money came through, plus an extra £750,000 as 'London Lighthouse has captured the public's imagination'.

I had my own reward. In the middle of the run, as I was holding the bucket in the lobby, an acquaintance told me about Section 28. This was a nasty, brutish measure intended to inhibit local authorities from subsidising lesbian and gay groups. In future it was to be illegal for them to 'promote homosexuality'.

Another cause, another emergency. Before I knew it, I was helping and, effortlessly, after forty-nine years of equivocation, I came out and said to anyone who was interested (and many who weren't) that I was gay. Since when, *my* life was transformed – but that's another story.

LYNDA LEE-POTTER

Lynda Lee-Potter, OBE, is the renowned (and controversial) columnist for the Daily Mail.
A former actress, she was named Columnist of the Year at the British Press Awards in 2000. In the same year, her semi-autobiographical novel Class Act *became a bestseller.*

actually, it's **love**

A Memorable Walk

My love affair with Dorset began over twenty years ago when we moved to live not far from the lost village of Tyneham on the Dorset coast. This green, wild and beautiful county is an integral part of my life. In winter I walk from Tyneham to the deserted beach at Worbarrow Bay. I skim pebbles across the tumultuous waves and think of the children who lived there and were so cruelly evicted in 1940.

Their parents were told that the Army needed their stunning bit of coastal England. The trusting villagers were taken out of their stone cottages and billeted in adjoining areas, often in crumbling outhouses and stables. The last villagers moved out in 1943 with a feeling of patriotism and thankfulness that they were helping to defend their country. They didn't know then that they would never return, that their cottages would crumble into ruins and their lovingly tended gardens would be overtaken by weeds. Never again were they to live in their enchanting village which reared strong and good people. If you grow up seeing only woods and green hills, towering cliffs and the sea lashing against the rocks, it is difficult to feel bad tempered or mean spirited. The government reneged on their promise and the villagers never returned, but, whenever I walk there, I feel their long-gone presence. The magnificent, unchanging landscape is uplifting and inspiring.

My son has been away from home for nearly two years cycling around the world and writing about his sometimes dangerous adventures. Yesterday he emailed me to say that he has seen wondrous lands, been treated with unbelievable kindness and had extraordinary experiences, but he yearns to return, to walk again in Dorset.

JAN ETHERINGTON

Jan Etherington, the award-winning radio and television comedy writer, is creator (with her husband, Gavin Petrie) of the comedy series Second Thoughts, Next of Kin, Duck Patrol *and* Faith in the Future *which won a British Comedy Award. They have written three series of their comedy* The Change *for BBC Radio 4.*

Teenage Crushers

When I recall the evening I was certain we'd be alone, I still wince. I was vamping precariously along the hall, wearing something diaphanous and balancing two chilled glasses of Sancerre when the front door opened and five sixteen-year-old boys exploded in. Only the fact that I was passing the broom cupboard at the time saved me from relinquishing forever my role as Sensible Parent and Figure of Considerable Authority.

Trying to hang on to your sex life when there are teenagers in the house requires the tenacity of a tax inspector and the ingenuity of a *Times* crossword compiler. When they were small, there were other problems, but at least they went to bed when it was dark. And even if they did get up again, you had a bit of warning – like a yell or a clunk as they fell out of the cot. Also, tiny kids don't know about rude bits, so, if they spotted you swinging from the chandelier while wearing a warm smile and a bit of tulle, they'd probably assume you were re-enacting a scene from *The Jungle Book*.

Teenagers know all about these things, making it more difficult to remain a woman of mystery. 'What's that?' enquired my daughter as I was sneaking something through the hall in a plain brown carrier bag.

'Just something I needed,' I said as I struggled with her, but she's stronger than I am.

'Ooh! Proper stockings,' she hooted, 'and a suspender belt!'

'It's a surprise for his birthday,' I said without thinking.

'Wouldn't he rather have a Leonard Cohen album?' she asked, but she knew what I meant.

And all this baloney about bringing a bit of spice back into your relationship. Eating in bed is almost impossible without running the assault course of your inquisitive offspring.

'Is this asparagus?'

'Yes.'

'Can we have some?'

'No.'

'Where are you going with it?'

'We're going to eat it in bed.'

'You're not ill, are you?'

'No.'

'I'm only allowed to eat in bed when I'm ill.'

Some of you who have been married a few years might be thinking, What's all this romance stuff? I have to explain that this was a new relationship and we were still very 'hands on'. I married for the second time when my son was thirteen and my daughter fifteen. I heard my daughter on the phone once. 'Yes, they're always snogging in the kitchen. God, it's embarrassing.'

My son exploded when he caught us in a clinch. 'Why can't you be a normal mother and not be in love?'

We never seemed to have an uninterrupted moment and teenagers like nothing better than being deliberately thick so that you have to spell everything out.

'We're having an early night,' I announce.

'Are you tired?' asks my son.

'You don't have to be tired to have an early night,' my daughter tells him knowingly.

And even when you think they've gone out, they come back.

'Mum? Where are you?'

Gasp for breath. 'In bed. Why, what's up?'

'Can I come in?'

Come in first. Knock later. 'Oh, sorry!'

'Can't you damn well knock before you barge in?'

'Sorry, I forgot to get some money for the club tonight.'

'We're trying to watch *Wildlife on One*!' I storm, attempting to disentangle myself from the duvet. It's not easy to be indignant and topless. Thank God we've got a television in the bedroom, otherwise I would have no excuse for my wantonness.

But why should I need an excuse? I'm not ready to

give up the pleasures of the flesh yet. So why do I have to apologise for a perfectly natural urge in what is still (in a darkened room with the light behind me) a relatively young woman?

Well, one of the reasons is that, when I was a kid, I couldn't imagine anyone over the ancient age of twenty actually placing themselves in a recumbent position with a person of the opposite gender and indulging in those practices we'd been told about in our hygiene class. My parents were openly affectionate, but kissing and holding hands were different from 'going the whole way'.

'Don't let boys rub against you,' bossy Eunice said firmly when we joined the local lads for ballroom-dancing classes. 'There could be consequences.'

I rushed home and looked up consequences. How could I protect myself from 'logical conclusions', I wondered.

So, although I insist I don't have any hang-ups about sex, I remember thinking how ludicrous it was to believe that grown-ups, who were obviously past any kind of emotion except unreasonable anger, should be indulging in an activity designed for the young. And as my children have always thought of me as a figure of fun, I'm sure they can't imagine anything dafter or more hysterical than their mother in the grip of passion. And yes, damn it, I was embarrassed when they caught me at it, or as near as caught me as makes no difference.

Even when they were miles away, they were still

indulging in the sport of *parentus interruptus*. One night, the phone rang. 'Mum, please can you pick me up from Woking? I've missed the last train ... Mum, are you OK?'

'I'm a bit out of breath. I had to run for the phone.' She knew damn well I wouldn't be running from anywhere but the bottom of the duvet at one in the morning.

One day, I realised that maybe I'd got the message across. We were watching the late film when I heard the Doc Marten boots of my daughter and her cronies clumping down the hall. 'Better knock,' I heard her whisper at the living-room door. 'They're probably at it on the sofa.' In those early years of my marriage, my teenage children made it clear that I was constantly letting them down and embarrassing them in front of their friends with unseemly displays of affection.

But that was then and this is now. Now I'm a grandmother and my daughter has a young daughter of her own. Daisy-Jude is not one to let attention wander from her needs and desires, even if Mummy and Daddy are 'night nights'. 'Piggy wants a cuddle, too,' is her most popular pre-dawn opener, as she thrusts a none-too-clean furry pig between her parents and clambers over them, into their bed, dragging an assortment of Lego and library books with her.

'We never get any time to ourselves,' moaned my daughter.

'Oh, dear,' I said, smiling.

GARY LINEKER

Gary Lineker, OBE, is one of the most famous names in the world of football. Former captain of England, he is now one of the nation's favourite TV personalities and is the lead presenter on BBC's Match Of The Day.

actually, it's **love**

Weather Report

Wherever I wander, wherever I roam,
  To Spain or Japan – where we once had a home,
I know it's peculiar, but number-one task
When phoning to England is always to ask,
For progress and news of the love of my life
(apart from my family, my sons and my wife),
When summer is here and rain's not stopped play,
What's the score from the CRICKET that day?

ALAN PLATER

Alan Plater is one of Britain's most respected writers, whose award-winning work has included the TV adaptation of The Barchester Chronicles, Beiderbecke, A Very British Coup *and* Last of the Blonde Bombshells.

actually, it's love

The Play's the Thing

Recently I read a review of my good friend Alan Bleasdale's funny and ferocious play *On the Ledge*, in which the critic said that Alan loved all his characters, especially the crazy ones; indeed, the crazier the people, the more Alan loves them.

The message from the critic was that this was wrong in some way I don't begin to understand. Why bother writing plays about people you can't stand? Even the villains I write about have some redeeming feature. Obadiah Slope, in *The Barchester Chronicles* – memorably played by Alan Rickman – was bearable because he was funny and got his comeuppance in the end. Like Malvolio in *Twelfth Night*, he is sick with self-love and there is no known cure for that condition. Slope would have done well in the 1980s and ended up with a knighthood or a prison sentence – possibly both.

We do everything for love if we have any sense. It generally takes root in adolescence. There are in the world several middle-aged women who, when they were girls at our school, provoked me into writing passionate poems about them. They never knew about either the passion or the poetry.

The poems were dreadful and I destroyed them all swiftly and mercilessly. They made E. J. Thribb seem like Shelley, and were densely packed with lines like 'Oh that we might walk life's highway hand in hand.' (Most of the lines began with 'Oh' – a very good reason for giving any poem directions to the nearest bonfire.)

Love was never just about girls. I was a Northerner, born in Jarrow and brought up in Hull. I love both places still, though Tyneside remains the country of my heart. Football has always been a central part of my family culture. At a rough estimate, I must have watched Hull City play about a thousand times. On an even rougher estimate the breakdown of the results is:

Won 333
Lost 333
Drawn 333
Goals for 999
Goals against 999

Viewed statistically, it has been a totally pointless exercise, which proves it must be true love.

It was in the adolescent period that another love affair started: with jazz. This is another incurable passion.

Curiously enough, it was caused by another type of love – filial. I loved my parents but needed something to rebel about – we had all seen the James Dean films, and rebellion became compulsory. Jazz was a way of rebelling against my parents without upsetting them too much. They were more concerned when I grew long sideboards hoping to look like Humphrey Lyttleton or Gerry Bowler, a fine and wacky Irish centre half who played briefly for Hull City with a Celtic abandon that couldn't survive the austere Humberside climate.

Now I'm bald, after the style of Shakespeare, with grown-up children who have kids of their own, and *that's* a love to cherish: love of grandchildren. You draw elephants and play daft games until you get tired or they get sticky, and then you hand them back to their parents. It is an ideal system.

All in all, it's a mighty catalogue, the things I've done for love: from standing in torrential rain watching a 0–0 draw between Hull City and Hartlepool United, to standing on one foot hearing the Ronnie Scott Quintet play to an audience of 400 in an auditorium with an official capacity of 150; from gazing in wonder at great comedians like Jimmy James and Norman Evans and ending up actually working with Sandy Powell, to drawing elephants for any small child who comes within range; from standing in cold December winds with ten other people in the belief that this would produce peace in Vietnam, to sitting in the gods at the Theatre Royal, Newcastle getting a stiff neck and a swift kick to the imagination watching Michael Hordern in *Twelfth Night*, the painful comedy that remains my favourite of Shakespeare's plays.

Shakespeare knew that you can't have laughter without tears, and by the same token you can't have love without the pendulum swinging into pain, despair and betrayal. If we write plays because we love our characters, it is also because we rage about what is done to them by society and its rulers. But all that belongs to another, more solemn agenda. We are here to celebrate love, lousy poems and all. I didn't *mean* to write rotten poems: I simply wasn't clever enough to write good ones. In any case, even a bad poem, a duff football match, an unfunny joke or a mediocre jazz band does no harm to the human race, which is more than you can say about the people who run the show most of the time.

Let us remember the gospel according to the great Duke Ellington who used to say to the audience at the end of each performance: 'You are very beautiful, very gracious, very talented and we want you to know that we do love you madly.'

CLARE BALDING

Clare Balding, sports commentator and journalist, is the BBC's highly regarded racing presenter. Formerly a leading amateur flat jockey and champion lady rider in 1990, Clare is an acknowledged expert in the racing world. She is also a Radio Five Live broadcaster and writes a regular column for the Observer.

actually, it's **love**

For the Love of Frank

Frank was the first one who really understood me. He would look at me with eyes full of knowledge, instinctively comprehending my fears and insecurities and would do his best to make me forget them. He was not handsome in the conventional sense: he had short spiky hair which refused to lie one way or the other, he had spots on his face and neck, and his skin was so sensitive that he had to have sun block plastered on his nose from spring until autumn. But he and I clicked and, for that reason alone, I thought he was the best-looking thing I had ever seen.

I was ten and Frank was about fourteen, although no one was really sure. He had been christened Prince, which I thought was a stupid name and, as he looked more like a rough street boy than either a pop star or a member of the royal family, Frank was infinitely more appropriate. When we were going 'posh', I would call him Prince Frank, smiling at the unsuitability of it all.

Frank was meant to be grey but he had brown ears

and black or brown splodges down his neck. He was what the horsey world refers to as a Heinz 57, which did not mean he was a can of baked beans but that he was made up of lots of different breeds. Walking proudly among the pure-bred ponies that the smarter children rode, I always felt that Frank and I were special. We were certainly different.

I would talk to him for hours as we rode around the countryside, and his brown ears would flicker appreciatively. I don't know whether he knew that he looked so odd, but he evidently thought that the other equine inhabitants of Park House Stables were not up to scratch. In particular, he hated the racehorses and treated them with the disdain of one destined for greatness. They might be in training for the Guineas or the Derby, but the spectacular heights of the Pony Club hunter trial awaited our Frank and he knew which he'd rather be running in.

He had a mouth with all the sensitivity of a block of wood, and would frequently go at least two strides faster than I wanted to at his fences. Showjumping was a game of hit and miss as far as he was concerned, and, as for dressage, well, that really was a waste of time. He did not think much of trotting round in circles, and the judges did not think much of him.

In the stable, Frank was adorable in a James Dean kind of way. He pretended he didn't care for kisses and cuddles, but really he enjoyed the attention. He always needed to be boss, though, and had an incurable habit of treading all over the toes of whoever was holding him. His favourite trick was to barge his way out of the stable, preferably taking in a foot or two en route, and gallop off, bucking and farting as he went. Even as I nursed my broken toes, I loved him.

I have never caused myself physical harm for the love of another being apart from Frank. An act of passion it was not; bloody painful it *was*. Frank and I had gone off riding one evening in search of my grandmother's lost whippet. It was a horribly rainy, cold night; Frank had been so good and had, for once, not run away with me, so I decided he shouldn't go out in the field. Instead I would make him a nice cosy bed in a warm stable and he could have a good night's sleep.

The trouble was that I was never much good at stable management. I picked up a pitchfork and stabbed it through a slice of straw. So far so good, except that I neglected to move my foot. The fork went right through the straw, my boot, my foot and into the ground. I pulled it straight out without fully understanding what I had done. I still have a scar on the top of my left foot and a smaller one on the underside. I think of them as the scars of my first true love.

COLIN DUNNE

*Colin Dunne, writer and journalist, contributes
to a variety of glossy magazines and is author of
several thrillers including* Black Ice *and*
Ratcatcher.

actually, it's **love**

A Short History of Dickie Bones

When I got into school the morning after my evening at Dickie Bones's flat, all the other boys gathered round. They were desperate to know. What had happened? What was his wife like? What had he said? 'Nothing much, bit boring,' I told them and, disappointed, they turned away. I was lying, of course. He'd changed my life.

I'd had a special claim on Dickie Bones ever since that first morning of term, when we'd finished our ritualistic 'Lord Receive Us With Thy Blessing', and I'd been the first to see him as he came loping up the long slope of the school drive.

'Hello, a native bearer,' he said, with a matey grin. 'I'm Richardson-Jones. Can you guide me to the art room?'

Even by the standards of art teachers, he was quite something: brown curls bubbling over ears and collar, cord trousers only half an inch away from being drainpipes, gaudy jacket and knitted tie. He wasn't like any teacher I'd seen before.

Our grammar school, in a cold northern market town, was as formal as a medieval church. The masters (teachers was far too flippant a word) were the high priests in their regalia of sports jackets and university ties, flannels and softly gleaming brogues. We were the peasants who got our Latin prep in on time, played rugby until our thighs were blue from blizzards, and whose most daring dissent was a cap tilted one degree off the obligatory horizontal. Masters did not smile at boys, matily or otherwise, they didn't say hello to them, and they certainly didn't talk in this easy, jokey way.

I sped back with the news. Sure enough, at the first art lesson, he didn't let me down. 'Right,' he said, 'let's get that ceiling down a bit. Black, d'you reckon, Dunne? What about the walls? Purple to bring that one in, yellow for the facing wall ...'

By the time we'd finished, the room looked like a fairground, and the whole school was buzzing with rumour that a wild man was among us.

Gentle, humorous, informal, he never even tried to teach; instead, he talked. He talked about the power of colour and shape, the emotion that fired a work of art, the frenzied lives of great artists, what they were trying to say when they picked up a brush, and we blossomed in the warmth of his passion like flowers in the sun. Before the week was out he was Dickie Bones.

His reputation grew, but we could never separate

rumour from reality. Was it true that the headmaster – a man who prided himself on beating a whole form alphabetically and still having made the last boy cry (Woods and Windles had a hard time at my school) – loathed Dickie Bones because he declined to attend school rugby games? Had he really once said he didn't believe in exams? Did he really have a wife like the women we had only seen on screen at the Plaza? Could it be possible that he played in a jazz band and drank in pubs?

What was even more extraordinary was the way he shattered the conventional understanding between boys and masters. Elsewhere, troublemakers were punished by being made to stay longer in the classroom, in detention. Since he considered that the greatest punishment was to be excluded from his lessons, Dickie Bones tossed them out. At first, for boys whose sole ambition was to escape from a classroom, this seemed splendid. Then, slowly, even the most stupid of them began to sense the shame of exile. They were missing out on something.

Every spare moment I had was spent in the art room, listening to Dickie Bones. I longed, I think, not so much for the skill of painting, which in my case was minimal, but for whatever mystery it was that he seemed to represent, which was a glimpse of a world that was full of excitement, drama and an outrageous glamour. Although I didn't know it then, he was a dissident, belonging to that distinguished elite who, from the Bohemians to today's Alternatives, see no merit in conforming.

'If you want to know how an artist sees the world, Dunne,' he said one day, 'get down to the library and ask for *The Horse's Mouth*.'

I read it to the end in one go, and then started at the beginning again. The novel by Joyce Cary, a brilliant and now sadly forgotten writer, showed me a life that knew no rules. It was also rude. When asked what he thought of modern art, the painter hero – if I remember correctly – said, 'It's rather like farting Annie Laurie through a keyhole – it's clever, but does it get you anywhere?'

The other boys were incredulous. A master had recommended a book which contained, in clear and undeniable print, the word 'farting'. These days it's probably on the school curriculum as a sport, but then it was dangerous stuff.

'Music, art, it's all the same, Dunne,' said Dickie Bones, packing me off to the library again, this time in search of *Mister Jelly Roll* by Alan Lomax, a book about Jelly Roll Morton, the New Orleans jazzman who played in a brothel. Our first-hand knowledge of brothels in the Yorkshire Dales was, in those days, limited, but I had a feeling that it beat the hell out of youth-club table tennis. In the local record shop, gathering dust on a shelf, I found my first 78. Across the 3,000 miles and the forty years that separated us, his Creole voice, anguished with rapture, cried, 'Ah, hellow Central, give me Doctor Jazz', and I was lost. Forever.

After that, under Dickie Bones's direction, came Steinbeck and, Hemingway and Faulkner, Greene and Waugh, and, when I wasn't painting, I was listening, and when I wasn't listening, I was reading. I was basking in reflected glory. After all, I had a special claim on him. I had seen him first. I was his native bearer. I was also, for the first time, top in art. Latin, French, English Lit … all of them fell by the wayside.

'Dunne,' wrote the headmaster in my report, 'appears to have taken up art at the expense of all his other studies. A characteristically perverse decision.' He predicted O-level failure in everything except art, a forecast which incited my father to hurl my report book across the room.

I didn't care. I was a rebel. I was Van Gogh Jelly Roll Dunne and I marched to a different drum.

Then, to my astonishment, came the invitation to his house. Because my pocket money, even inflated with paper-round wages, only allowed for four new records a year, my collection was a little slow in growing. 'Come round and listen to some records, Dunne,' he said. To his house? Yes. Me? Yes. To a master's? It was all too heady.

When I got there, I had my tie undone and my socks wrinkled to show that I too belonged to the rule-breakers, farters, brothel clients and famous writers who lived for their art and were prepared to risk wearing a shirt without a name tag. As I went in, I saw, hanging on the wall, a trombone. Did he really play in a band? Oh, he said, he used to, but he didn't have much time these days. I was inside the house of a genuine jazzman.

'Do you drink beer?' he asked.

At fifteen, I had once had a shandy on holiday. 'Quite a bit, actually,' I said, striving to give the impression that I poured the stuff over my cornflakes.

'Bring Colin a beer,' he called through to the kitchen as he put on a record of 'SOL Blues' by Louis Armstrong. 'Know what SOL stands for?' he asked. 'Shit Outta Luck.'

I was inside the house of a genuine jazzman who called me by my first name and had just said shit.

All the time I was trying to keep my eyes off a huge portrait over the mantelpiece of a beautiful woman who was, it appeared to me with little expertise in this area, to be naked. Dickie Bones was the first to mention it. He hadn't got the set of the neck quite right, he said, although the set of the neck seemed one of its least interesting features. My experience of naked women was at the same level as my drinking.

I was inside the house of a genuine jazzman who called me by my first name, said shit and was talking about naked women.

At that moment, the door opened and in came a very beautiful woman indeed, bearing my beer (in, I now realise, something the size of a sherry glass), and she smiled at me and said hello. I stammered, I stuttered, I wriggled, and my face glowed, a beacon of embarrassment. It was his wife. It was also the woman in the picture. Try as I could, as she handed me my beer, I could not see this pleasant woman modestly clad in shirt and skirt, but only the naked body on the wall.

I was inside the house of a genuine jazzman who called me by my first name, said shit, and I was drinking beer handed to me, for all intents and purpose, by a naked woman.

He talked of books and writers and music and painting, although, for once, rendered mute by ecstasy, I took little of it in. In the Yorkshire Dales in those days, a nude, a beer and Louis Armstrong were every bit as potent as sex, drugs and rock 'n' roll to a later generation.

The next day I realised, a little sadly, that, if I told the truth at school, no one would believe me. 'Nothing much, bit boring,' I said, and they drifted away. There was another reason too that had nothing to do with credibility: it was all far too precious to share.

When the exam results came in, I passed everything except art. 'I told you exams are a waste of time,' said Dickie Bones. We sang 'Lord Dismiss Us With Thy Blessing' and left. When we came back the next term, Dickie Bones had gone too. The headmaster smiled when he made the announcement. Desolate as I felt, I still knew he had changed me. Doors had been opened which now could never be closed.

Dickie Bones taught me about love. Love of painting, love of music, love of books and, yes, I suppose, love of beer and naked ladies and breaking rules. His lesson wasn't about art at all: it was about the love of life. Every time I hear that voice wail 'Ah, hellow Central, give me Doctor Jazz', I think about him.

Thanks, Dickie Bones.

PHILLIP SCHOFIELD

Phillip Schofield, actor and one of the UK's favourite radio and TV presenters, is currently hosting This Morning, Test The Nation *and* Winning Lines *with the National Lottery. He won theatrical acclaim playing the Doctor in the award-winning* Dr Dolittle.

actually, it's **love**

Shakespeare in Love

One hot summer night, many years ago, I took a girl-friend to see *The Comedy of Errors* at Regent's Park open-air theatre. We had a wonderful evening, and, as we walked back across the park, she said that she loved the sound of Shakespeare. It made her go weak at the knees. That was it, the challenge was on. Later that night, I remembered that I had an old scratchy LP with a recording of Peter Sellers on the Michael Parkinson show. He had performed a little bit of Richard III: 'Now is the winter of our discontent ...' and so on. I decided that would do the trick. So for the remainder of the night I played it over and over again, until I had it by heart. At six in the morning I went to bed tired but extremely pleased with myself, ready to try it out on her the following evening. It's funny how these things stick in your head. I can still remember it to this day.

And did it work? Of course it did!

DEREK MALCOLM

*Derek Malcolm is the former film critic of
the* Guardian. *He was president of the Film
Critics Association, and a governor of the British
Film Institute. In a distinguished career he has
also written* Bollywood: Popular Indian Culture,
A Century of Films *and, most recently,*
Family Secrets.

actually, it's **love**

The Passion of Malcolm

If the greatest expression of love is a willingness to endure pain for others, as Mel Gibson seemed so sure about in *The Passion of the Christ*, then my first love is my dog. Well, maybe he is my third love since I have a wife and daughter, but then they do not cause me quite the same kind of purgatorial torture.

Bruno is a rough-haired, light-coloured Labrador who makes me feel bad at least six times a day and probably more. I'm not sure whether he means to, but the fact is that he does.

First off, why is his breakfast late? Second, for heaven's sake, when will he get his morning walk? Third, what the hell am I doing pottering about with the lunch I don't give him instead of taking him out in the afternoon too? Fourth, why do I leave him in the car for hours when (a) shopping, (b) going to a restaurant or (c) seeing friends who don't like dogs. Fifth, when I get back from these useless expeditions, why do I not always bring him back something to eat? And sixth, when the hell is he going to get his pee-stroll before bedtime?

And then, of course, there is the worst thing of all: going away on holiday without him. There's a nice man at the kennels and plenty of other dogs with sniffable backsides, but to Bruno it is a dereliction of duty second to none. On this score, I have some friends whose beloved dog, about whom the husband had even written a book, suddenly died. I recently asked them how they had survived the traumatic experience. They had been, they said, utterly devastated for at least a month. But now they had a sense of freedom they hadn't experienced for years. They could actually go away together without a worry at the back of their minds.

Make no mistake, I don't want that freedom yet awhile, since I genuinely love the big, fat mutt who stands in front of me staring with his mute requests, day in, day out. He has not only got a beautiful face but, despite his faults, a beautiful if impatient nature too. He never growls or bites, and only barks at the postman. He gives me and my wife untold affection, even when we have let him down utterly by leaving him at home alone. When we come back, he is beside himself with joy. His apparent love for us is as hopelessly complete as our love is for him. But what a menace all the same. I know this is silly. Animals are not human and shouldn't have human feelings projected upon them. But unfortunately dogs are convinced they are human and expect the bloody lot. The problem is that, whatever you do for them, you never think it is quite enough. And if I hear my wife say 'poor boy' once more, just because he wants his meal half an hour earlier than usual, I think I shall just give up.

Unfortunately, the whole thing gets worse with age – mine, not Bruno's. Because the more I see of the way we treat 'dumb' animals, especially for eating purposes, the more guilty I feel for not doing right by my cosseted dog. He is sleeping now, thank goodness. But any moment he will be down from upstairs, wagging for a walk or a biscuit, or preferably both.

I believe that the way we treat animals in general has a direct bearing on how we treat our fellow human beings. And I don't like that either. Sometimes I do daft things, like getting wet and cold and miserable just to satisfy the mutt's desire to splash about in the mud in winter, which plays total havoc with the back seat of my once-smart car on the way back.

And the other day, I told a farmer off for leaving a horse alone in a muddy, grassless winter field for three months solid, apparently without exercise. Horses get lonely too, I said. He was not impressed. He's fed every day, he said. But two days later the horse was no longer there. One hopes he took the point. But he'd probably eaten it.

Yes, love to me means guilt as well as a lot of other things, perhaps because I watched my father die in a ghastly nursing home because I couldn't possibly have him with me in my flat, as he wanted so badly. Medically, it was impossible. Also, my hours as a journalist made it doubly hopeless. Perhaps I am projecting this, and other things, on to Bruno.

Oh God, here he is, wagging hopefully. A biscuit won't suffice. He demands his walk, and it's raining cats and dogs.

THE DUCHESS OF YORK

Reflecting her many interests and life experiences, The Duchess of York has authored an impressive number of books on a broad variety of subjects. Among her adult titles are: The Duchess's best-selling autobiography, My Story; *a thoughtful collection of essays entitled,* What I Know Now: Simple Lessons Learned the Hard Way *and an art book of the Duchess's landscape photography,* Moments, *which she recently published to benefit her London-based foundation,* Children in Crisis. *The Duchess also co-authored two historical books:* Victoria and Albert: Life at Osborne House, *and* Travels with Queen Victoria, *as well as five books with Weight Watchers about healthy food and lifestyle. The Duchess is an internationally popular children's book author, having created and published series about* Budgie the Little Helicopter, The Adventures of Amanda, *and most recently* The Adventures of Little Red.

Friends for Life

The love I give to my children and the love they show in return is something quite unique. I still cannot quite believe the magical blessing of children. How is it that only nine months of pregnancy can produce such miracles that develop into the greatest friends you could ever have?

My children tell me the truth about myself, and of course at times you do not like their frankness but then love is unconditional.

They hug me when I feel blue and make me smile when life seems in despair. There is a freshness and sincerity in their faces which always reassures me. So, for me, what I do for love is to nurture my two beautiful children because in return they enrich and lighten my life.

DALIP TAHIL

Dalip Tahil, major star of Indian theatre and cinema, got his first acting break in the Oscar-winning film Gandhi. *In India he won plaudits for his roles in the television series* Buniyaad *and* Qayamat Se Qayamat Tak. *More recently he has appeared in London in the stage musical* Bombay Dreams, *and as Dan Ferreira in* EastEnders.

actually, it's **love**

A Different Mountain

There's a lot I remember about the school I went to in Nainital, a beautiful town in the hills in the north of India. I was sent there from my home in Bombay to study. My father was in the air force, my mother was the most wonderful and stable woman in my life, but school was to be in Nainital. Most people think of Nainital as the place that has, at its heart, a quite breathtaking lake or heart-lurching views of the snow-capped Himalayas, and they are right. But for me it was also the place that changed my life and handed me the start of a love affair that has lasted all my life.

A love affair with acting.

That year at school, when I was thirteen, also taught me something about love. It can take you in all sorts of directions and maybe not the one you wanted to go in, but, if it does, you should wait and see, not despair, because it might lead to something better.

Let me explain. I remember the school, Sherwood College – a Church of England boys' school – for lots of reasons. It is known as one of the oldest boarding schools in India, but I remember it was run with a firm but kindly discipline by a delightful man. Reverend Llewellyn, he was called, now retired and living back in England. I also recall Mr Luther, my English teacher – but I'll come to him in a moment. Most of all I remember the excitement that led up to Founders Day, and in particular the annual climbing expedition that all boys from my year onwards embarked upon twenty-five days before the big day. It was that which changed the course of my life.

All students had to be involved in some way on that special day, but this trip was the one we all knew we had to be on. It was the sixties, and we dreamed of being given the freedom that young men at that time thought was the height of ambition: sitting around in the sun, growing our hair long and arriving back at school to a hero's welcome. The climb was, after all, a real test of stamina and endurance, and you had to work hard to prove you were fit enough and capable enough to join in.

I couldn't wait. Neither could anyone else. I was thirteen, and the height of the climb they were aiming to achieve on Nanda Bhana was hoped to be more than they had managed the year before.

Nothing else at that time mattered to me. I was selected, and was in seventh heaven. And then, two days before the big day, disaster loomed. My throat felt sore, my limbs ached. I lay in bed in my dormitory before the departure telling no one how I felt because I knew I would be stopped from going. The memory of how I dragged myself on to the school bus that took us on the four-hour journey to the start of the climb is a blur. I was far too ill by then to concentrate.

And of course I was spotted. How could I not be? A thirteen year old looking as though he had possibly less than a heartbeat between him and death's door is not hard to spot. I pleaded, I begged, I cried. But there was no decision anyone could make except to send me back to school. They were kind, but firm. I would jeopardise the whole trip. They couldn't make the climb with me in that state.

Miserably I went back to school. I was put to bed and, several days later, I emerged from the sickbay, shattered, still disconsolate, but fit again. At thirteen you bounce back. But I had nothing to contribute to Founders Day. Everyone else did. And then, as I roamed the school grounds feeling dejected, I bumped into Mr Luther, my English teacher, who clearly felt sorry for me.

'Look,' he said, 'I haven't cast everyone in the school play for Founders Day. Why don't you read for one of the parts?'

My acting experience up till then had been a single appearance in the school nativity play. I wondered, hopefully, if he had remembered that, but I suspect his motive was purely a compassionate one. Or, even more possible, my English was better than the other choices he had at the time. I did not delude myself.

The play was a comedy called *My Three Angels* and I was asked to read for Joseph. I was not aware of it at the time but it was one of the leads and, to my amazement, I got it. Not only did I get it, but also the strangest thing happened. Even though I didn't understand all the words, I became hopelessly involved in the part. It was not just a question of wanting to do well so that I could contribute to Founders Day, I was gripped with an overwhelming, instinctive feel for what I was doing. It captivated me – I don't think obsession is too strong a word – and there was no going back.

That year I won the Kendal's Cup for Acting. Not only was it unique in the school's history for someone to win the cup with only one acting role to their credit, but the added prestige for an aspiring actor was that the cup was donated by Geoffrey and Laura Kendal, parents of Felicity Kendal. One of my fondest memories of Sherwood College is being asked – indeed, *allowed* – to carry Geoffrey Kendal's bags when he came to the school with their famous Shakespeareana touring company.

So now I look back and wonder what it would have been like if I had not caught flu, and had gone on that mountaineering trip. I know I would have enjoyed it, but I might never have found my real passion in life. Now I know that, whatever life throws at me, if something is *meant* to be, it *will* be; and that, no matter what the setbacks and the trials of life, one way or another I will always be acting.

GLENDA JACKSON

Glenda Jackson, CBE and Member of Parliament, is also a twice Oscar-awarded actress for her roles in Women in Love *and* A Touch of Class. *In 1992 she gave up her hugely successful career when she was elected Labour MP for Hampstead and Highgate. She has been a member of the Mayor of London's Advisory Cabinet on Homelessness since 2000.*

actually, it's love

Management Material

I have no interest whatsoever in football, despite my claims to support Tranmere Rovers.

This claim has nothing to do with the beautiful game, but my resentment at the automatic assumption that my Merseyside antecedents mean a blind loyalty to either Liverpool or Everton. Liverpudlians like to pretend that my Merseyside birthplace – Birkenhead – doesn't exist. Well it does.

However, I digress.

One day my son, aged seven or eight (he is now thirty-five), arrived home from school and informed me that I was the manager of his newly formed five-a-side football team. With an aplomb which in retrospect causes me no small amazement, I thanked him and asked what the duties and responsibilities of such an awesome office entailed.

I can't remember what he said, but I can remember what I did.

Twice a week, six or seven healthy, energetic and

incredibly noisy male children would pile into my really rather small car to be chauffeured by me to their destination: Wednesdays to their training session, Saturdays to the match. And, of course, training and/or match over, they were chauffeured home.

There were, in addition, secretarial and cheerleader duties, complete with oranges carefully quartered and eagerly accepted by small, invariably muddy and sweaty footballers, when half-time came around. Being cheerleader was not a solitary occupation. All matches produced parents in abundance and some of these 'adults' took winning or losing – in my team's case, the latter, somewhat regularly – far too seriously.

The team stayed and played together for several seasons. Their enthusiasm for muddy, Arctic-wind-swept fields never wavered. Mine never existed, but I don't think the teams – mine or their competitors – would ever have known.

In mud and rain, chapped lipped and with chilblained toes and fingers, I stood week after week shouting encouragement, criticising the ref, passing out the oranges, consoling and extolling as the result demanded, pretending I understood the offside rule and praying for the final whistle just to get out of the cold.

When the team decided they were too old to be shepherded around by a woman – nine-year-old boys can be so cruel – I took their rejection bravely. It was not that hard to admire their independent spirits while hiding a broken heart – well, *they* believed me. The things we do for love, indeed.

FRANK DELANEY

Frank Delaney, acclaimed Irish writer and broadcaster is the bestselling author of My Dark Rosaleen, The Sins of the Mothers, Telling the Pictures *and* Pearl. *His latest book is* Ireland: A Novel.

actually, it's love

Family Matters

Realistically, the things we do for love mostly have nothing to do with romance. We contribute our loving in a tight enough circle of children, parents, long-term partners and their relatives. To these, our history of undemonstrativeness and restraint allows us to make expressions of love along a scale from tender to respectful. In most other ways we restrict: expressions of love, however non-romantic, are not permitted to colleagues, neighbours or, most regrettably, siblings.

The thing I did for love attacked this spore in our emotional culture, but I did not know I was doing it, and only now can I see it with any clarity: as with the old Box Brownie cameras of childhood, the negative has taken a long time to develop.

I grew up as a child of the two deadly Cs, Calvinism and Catholicism, that so inhibited our feelings in the north-west of Europe. The youngest boy of a large family, I eventually, wordlessly, watched the youngest girl die of cancer in her early forties: she was ten years older than me. Although it was not my first bereavement by death – my father had died several years earlier – it was, and remains, my most important and powerful. It comes back to me frequently, not through the natural sadness of it, or the terrible poignancy – she had five children and the dearest of natures – but through what it taught me about the L-word.

At the funeral, something odd had surfaced inside me, a curious sense of self-importance in all the confusion. Obviously I stifled it, afraid of that baser kind of egoism with which overbearing people appropriate family events. And there seemed no reason why any unusual intensity should apply. We had had no more than a fairly 'ordinary' relationship, similar to those of all families I thought I knew. She lived in Britain, I in Dublin, and we met only once every two years or so. However, warmth had always run between us.

The emotion I felt at the graveside so puzzled and threw me that I began to return to it long afterwards, and gradually I figured out that, far from being a rabid kind of self-centredness, this was a formative component. A 'life event' had happened to me, and I could learn from it, grow under its instruction.

This slow realisation may have been some kind of delayed shock, some strange, postponed mourning. When I finally let it out of its box, every texture of the funeral then rushed back at me, and with it a new and searing set of affections for my dead sister's face. Everywhere. From a taxi window, a girl who walked like her; heard on the radio, a rarely played Gracie Fields song that she had whacked out on the piano with a fair imitation of Gracie's leathery sinuses; met a man with three sons who each had names my sister had given her boys, my nephews; found in a book a birthday card she sent me when I was twenty; and in the bottom of a suitcase a handkerchief she had given me many years earlier. All this happened within one week, but it was now eight years since she died.

When I interrogated this sudden, delayed remembering, I wondered whether it had come on with a rush simply because something within me decided it was time to let go. Or was this unfinished business? I had wept enough at the time – or so I thought.

One day's events in particular overwhelmed me. The morning contained nothing to warn me: no party, nor woman-row the night before, none of that inexplicable gloom when I woke up; and at the other end of the scale, no sign of the more dangerous foe, elation.

In a noon of glorious sunshine, I left a village in north Wales where I was doing some research and caught the train for London. By the time I reached the dining car, I was close to tears, to this day a completely unusual situation – I too have the locker-room credentials of all men of my generation from these islands.

64

Several exercises prove useful in such situations: recall the list of tasks facing me when I get back to London; make a note to check with my secretary as to whether A, B and C need any further attention; was the VAT inspection agreed? Thus, the iron of mundanity seeped into the soul.

The mettle snapped after lunch when I settled to the crossword. Two clues, I cannot recall them precisely but they may have been something like 'Gracie Fields's favourite houseplant' and 'egg container'. The answers were 'aspidistra' and, savagely, 'ovaries'. This word lashed out even though the details of my sister's illness were kept from me by the daft secrecies of this emotionally maladroit family system that large Irish Catholic families have. Ovaries have to do with procreation, and procreation has to do with sex.

In order to compose myself I used another old business trick. I wrote down at random an intensifying progression of queries, in order to try and edit down to one question, and thereby get close to one answer, a kind of homing in on the nucleus of the problem. Like a rare game of patience it all came out. Why had the passage of time not erased this dreadful, bereft feeling?

The answer distilled reluctantly to four letters on the page – that word again, a word I never heard in my ordinary family growing up in the Irish countryside, not even once. 'Love' in my background was as taboo an expression as any of the usual four-letter ones. In my time, fathers did not 'love' their sons; parents didn't 'love' their children, not where I came from. Siblings didn't 'love' each other. No such thing. Stuff, if not nonsense. Nobody was to blame; that was the way of the world.

The rest became immediately apparent. I had never 'loved' my sister, therefore I never mourned her. Obviously, all the sudden recollections of her had come – that is to say, I only began to mourn her fully – when, eight years after her funeral, some part of me acknowledged that it was all right to use the word 'love'.

Anger broke out, followed by a sense of shame at coming from a national society where such familial reticence was the norm. It calmed down soon, but I have never seen any family relationship in the same light since. All such withholdings of love gouge flaws as deep as geological faults in all families who have them.

My sister whom I now love (note: *love* with no quotation marks), my dead sister, who had cancer finally in every available organ of her body, informs much that I do. In two long novels and a novelette I have been unable not to represent her in some way, and the novel I am writing at the moment will be suffused with the loving principles I was never told about, and was never allowed by the general culture to practise when she was alive.

But I try to practise them now – even if I, like most people, still have difficulty in getting the words along that difficult, often taboo-blocked canal from the heart to the lips. If we love someone, we should tell them.

Why not? Dr Johnson, an Englishman to the tacks in the soles of his boots, and therefore by definition stiff rigid in the upper lip, was able, in the eighteenth century, to lunge across a London dining table to a man he had but recently met and say warmly, 'Give me your hand, sir, for I have taken a liking to you.'

Terrific. Brave! I am with him all the way – even if it means unsound tear ducts whenever I hear a cracked recording of 'The Biggest Aspidistra in the World'.

MELANIE CANTOR

Melanie Cantor, one of the UK's most established agents and publicist for a host of top television presenters, lives in London with her two teenage sons. Earlier this year she presented her own successful TV show for Channel 4, Making Space, *but continues to enjoy her day job.*

actually, it's **love**

Love in the Balance

The darkness was stirred by the sound of his breathing. Gentle and regular. So reassuring. I stood there, staring at the outline of his head, not wanting to move for fear of disturbing him and yet desperate to lie down next to him and hold his warm body in my arms, wrap my love around him and feel the warmth of his sweet breath on my face. But he needed his sleep, and I was not going to be the one to enrage him with my selfish desire for loving reassurance.

The depth of my emotion almost shocked me. I would never have believed it was possible to love another human being so much. It overwhelmed my heart, filling it with equal measure of joy and fear: the joy of knowing such deep intense love, and the fear of losing it. The fear of losing him. Such an irrational thought and yet one that inhabited a permanent corner of my head, constantly drawing me into his room to check that he was there, breathing, safe.

And yet, even though I loved him more than anyone I

had ever loved before, somehow I had willingly made the choice to bring someone else into our relationship. Why? Was it foolhardiness? Was it greed, or complacency? Why destroy something so extraordinary? And this was my dilemma. I stood watching him sleep, wondering whether anything would ever be the same again. I loved this person so much, and yet somehow I believed I was capable of loving another in equal measure. Or did I? Was this just a selfish conviction to justify my maternal lust. For tomorrow, my second child would be born and my heart would have to learn to divide itself in half between two little people. Would it be possible?

Sixteen years later and ... yes, it was.

ANTHONY ANDREWS

Anthony Andrews, award-winning actor, shot to fame as Sebastian Flyte in Brideshead Revisited, *winning a Golden Globe and a BAFTA. More recently he appeared in London to much acclaim as Professor Higgins in* My Fair Lady. *He is also the highly appreciated host of ROC's fund-raising concerts.*

actually, it's love

Why I Love Malcolm McDowell

I was depressed. Very depressed. I had no qualifications, no prospects and I was flat broke. I'd had enough of sweeping stages and making tea.

Young, ambitious and deeply desirous of a theatrical career and a serious relationship (though not necessarily in that order), I had returned to the environment that had first inspired me and supported my dreams some years previously: the Chichester Festival Theatre. Here, at least, I found a number of like-minded souls working as the stage crew, all seasonal labourers and students of the art, and from all walks of life. It was a veritable hotbed of tirelessly determined testosterone.

One sunny morning it was Bob Selby, the kindly production manager, who suggested that I should get myself to London without delay. He had heard on the grapevine that the auditions for the new Alan Bennett play had hit a few snags and, although he couldn't guarantee it, he had a hunch that I might relieve the itch in the vocational department, public-school types being a little thin on the ground as most were nose to the grindstone at university if they had any sense.

Dear Bob was quite right. Some weeks later I was plucked from obscurity and thrown together with a fascinating motley group of twenty would-be actors in a rehearsal room in the bowels of the great Theatre Royal Drury Lane. We became the chorus of naughty schoolboys who supported John Gielgud, Alan Bennett and Paul Eddington among others in Alan's wonderful play *Forty Years On*. It was the kindling of a long love affair with the theatre.

So far so good, one might say, but my meteoric transition was far from smooth. London accommodation was the next hurdle. Thankfully there were several friends whose floors I could all too often crash out on after exhausting searches for digs. One such, Alan Warren, was playing one half of Lady Sybilline Quarrell (Lady Ottoline Morrell) in the show, wearing a long flowing gown that disguised the fact that he was perched precariously on my shoulders. (I used to plead with him not to eat beans at the pre-show gatherings at the adjacent greasy spoon.)

Alan actually provided a real spare bed on the nights he was not 'entertaining' after the show, and many is the time that I would find myself all tucked up staring at the wall above that bed that bore many of the 'faces' of our time. For Alan was not a newcomer to the theatre: he had been very successful as a child in all manner of shows, and consequently had developed a very lucrative second income as photographer to the great and not so great, all of whom needed their headshots in order to be in the market at all.

The treasured spare bed was in the room that doubled as the studio, and Alan took care to make certain that only the most famous or the most attractive adorned the wall. It was a sweet repose, and I would often fantasise about meeting those who stared down at me during the night.

One face in particular would haunt my dreams. Georgina Simpson, a young, upwardly mobile and stunning young starlet, was photographed very seductively lying stretched out on a leopard-skin rug. I made up my mind that my life as I had always wanted it to be could never truly begin until we had met. I would imagine how that great event would occur. We would meet regularly and in all sorts of glamorous places: it was always love at first sight and always perfect.

In reality, of course, things were tougher, much tougher. Alan, for all his regular promises, had completely failed to contact her, and my constant reminders were wearing very thin indeed when, one evening after a performance, my luck changed. I was as usual the last one out of the dressing room, on the very top floor of the Apollo Theatre in Shaftsbury Avenue. I was in no particular hurry to finish attending to the acne and blocked pores, exacerbated by months of liberally applied five-and-nine greasepaint. After all, there was little to rush out for except the usual saga of exactly whose floor I was to avail myself of that night.

Suddenly I could hear Alan calling my name and furiously climbing back up the stone staircase that led from the stage door. On arrival he threw open the door and panted, 'She's in the pub, move yourself!'

Panic. Lots of aftershave and panic, but shortly afterwards, sweaty and shaking, there I was leaning across the bar desperately attempting to appear frightfully cool and nonchalant. 'What'll it be?' I fumbled in my pocket in an attempt to find any remains of the eighteen pounds we were paid every week. The goddess turns, looks me up and down, and says, 'No thanks, I've got one.' And that was that. All my dreams dashed by the stupidity of the opening line. Then she left, surrounded by the hip and the cool, royally attended by those with a vocabulary. Gone, perhaps forever. Or was she?

A year later things had changed quite significantly. I had found somewhere to live for the remainder of the run of the show. A rather Parisian (or what I *thought* to be Parisian) flat in the roof space of a crumbling block right in the centre of Soho, it was literally a stone's throw from the stage door. However, the rent was a crippling ten pounds a week, and the show was now closed.

To cheer me up, my dear sister Janet would often take pity on me. She was working in a pub in Grafton Street,

Victoria, usually frequented by theatricals, comics and the like. We would often while away the slower nights over a half of bitter shared between two glasses, simply face-spotting; occasionally she would hear of a party and if she had no date we went together.

On one such night there was an event happening way up in north London in some rather obscure new disco club. There was talk of a plethora of celebrities and free drinks. Janet was reluctant – the only way to get there was for her to fork out for the bus – but luck was with us and, though she was very dubious about his motives, a friend in the bar offered a lift.

On arrival, there was very little to recommend the joint. It was very dark, damp and smelly, hardly a soul to be seen, and the promised 'one free drink' took an interminable time to arrive. It was almost as if the management already smelled the first faint odour of failure. It turned out to be a birthday party for Sal Mineo, an actor who had become famous in a movie called *Exodus*, and we were all assured that many illustrious names would appear. Eventually the place attracted one or two more folk as the restaurants and theatres emptied, and the staff made several attempts to wheel in a giant birthday cake while the theme music to the film was played very loudly. Each of these attempts was aborted as the owner decided to wait for the big names to appear. None did.

Gradually one's eyes became accustomed to the

darkness … and then it happened. Way off in the gloom, on the far side of the dance floor, I saw her. The truly amazing part was that she saw me too! We both seemed to stare for ages in amazement. Could it be? Yes it could. Georgina Simpson was sitting there staring at me and even occasionally smiling. My heart was in my mouth. She must really like the look of me to keep returning my glances. Finally Janet had had enough of the love-sick looks being exchanged across the room and practically threw me off my seat: tired of encouraging me, she forced the move.

I stood up, I was en route. Georgina stood up too. Slowly, heart pounding, I crossed the floor. She did the same. Now I knew I was in love. Could this really be happening? It was the beginning of the famous dance-hall scene in *West Side Story*. We met right in the middle of the floor. Then abruptly she stopped, squinted at me rather peculiarly with her head on one side, and quite suddenly she frowned. 'Oh my God! I thought you were Malcolm McDowell.'

God bless you, Malcolm. I would never have been able to come up with an opening line. We married a year later.

SIR RICHARD BRANSON

Sir Richard Branson, entrepreneur, world-class balloonist and adventurer, owns 150 companies in twenty-nine countries including Virgin Atlantic Airways, as well as being trustee of several charities.

actually, it's **love**

That Sinking Feeling

I met this lovely lady who worked as an assistant in a bric-a-brac store. The only way her boss would allow me to come and see her was if I bought something every time I visited. The courting and visits went on for ninety days, and my houseboat finally sank from the weight of the many items of bric-a-brac I had bought from the store. Still, this lovely lady felt rather responsible and once it was dried out agreed to move in with me. Two equally lovely children followed – worth every bit of bric-a-brac.

BRYAN FORBES

Bryan Forbes, the multi-talented actor, director and writer, has won acclaim as the director of The Stepford Wives, Séance On A Wet Afternoon *and* Whistle Down The Wind, *while his screenwriting credits include* The Angry Silence *and* The League of Gentlemen. *He is the author of some ten novels. This extract is from his autobiography,* A Divided Life.

actually, it's **love**

A Passionate Journey

The Blitz was over and we were allowed to return home during the holidays. My parents had found another house in Newbury Park near Ilford in Essex.

I can remember nothing of that first holiday, I can only recall the return to Cornwall. I caught the train back at Paddington, not labelled and dragooned as on the first occasion, not in fear of the falling bombs, but as somebody going back to familiarity after a break.

I occupied the same carriage as a ravishing young school girl, like me a returning evacuee, who wore the brown mortar board of a convent school and who proved to be just as vulnerable as myself. She was journeying to Newquay and destined to leave the train before me to catch another connection. Her name was Marguerite and I fell immediately and helplessly in love with her.

Love in one's youth is an endless purple passage and to attempt to disguise that fact is to deny the beauty and agony of a perfection that comes but once, for, to turn to Connolly: *'once only are we perfectly equipped for loving:*

we may appear to ourselves to be as much in love at other times – so does a day in early September, though it is six hours shorter, seem as hot as one in June.'

Was I 'perfectly equipped' for loving? I thought I was. The first and most urgent fear that possessed me, the fear that the homing journey would come to an end before I had managed to make the force of my emotion felt, was soon dispelled. We were told at Exeter that the train had to be diverted – there had been a bad crash on the main line between there and Plymouth, with the consequent delay of some hours.

I am compelled to warn those who are now expecting to read a variation of Frank Harris or *Walter's Secret Life* that, unlike those two sexual athletes, I did not fall upon the delectable Marguerite the moment the train pulled out of Exeter. I wish I had, for one of the keenest pangs of advancing middle age is the remembrance of chances lost. My thoughts were totally impure, my motives towards her unashamedly carnal, but I lacked that first requisite of the would-be seducer – opportunity. We did not have the carriage to ourselves. Being wartime it was crammed to overflowing.

I should perhaps anticipate my reader's curiosity and reveal that the attraction was mutual. Although I can understand my own feelings, since I want this to be an honest account of my life and tribulations, I cannot comprehend why the enchanting Marguerite gave me a second glance. Studying the Box Brownie snapshots of the period, I appear to have been something less than God's gift to convent girls. I had an absurd haircut and a perky little face devoid of character. I looked rather like one of the dust-jacket illustrations to Richmal Crompton's *Just William* series.

But apparently I helped to pass the journey for her and, oblivious to the other occupants of the carriage, we embarked on the first tentative voyage of exploration which only erotic liars pretend to recall in detail. I have no such details, alas; I cannot remember a single word we exchanged, all I retain is the picture, blurred around the edges, of a young girl trapped within that building grove of Proust's imagination, who indulged me, made me captive, enchanted and destroyed me and who now still has the power to rekindle the ashes of a lost personality.

She was, unlike any girl I had encountered before, soft in outline, with that pampered loveliness that comes but once. I began to make feverish plans, carrying on incoherent conversations which never began or ended, while my mind evolved the most fantastic schemes. With every passing minute I became more and more conscious of the need to declare myself before it proved too late. But at fourteen the words don't come. First love can only be expressed in retrospect, and even then the middle-aged poet distorts the past with experience. At the time it is a race towards a winning post that never gets nearer, a waking nightmare.

Somehow, I must have found the courage to ask for her address. I have no doubt that she was more in command of the situation than I was, for girls of that age are infinitely more aware. Even then I must have had some inner conviction that my pen would prove mightier than my spoken word.

We eventually arrived at Exeter. She left the train there and I journeyed on alone to Helston. I imagined her arrival at Newquay, tried, like any other young lover before me, to put myself in her place. I went over every inch of my own battlefield, cross-examined and reviled myself for the stupidity of my manoeuvres, cursed my timid nature. I became convinced that all was lost, that she would never think of me again.

The moment I was back in the vicarage I made the long journey an excuse to retire early. Secure in my own room, the door locked, I put pen to paper and wrote my first love letter. I recall that for her part she had given me a *poste restante* address, for her incoming mail was intercepted and censored by the nuns. I think I wrote to her care of a local newsagent.

The new term began the following day, but all was dross. I had posted my letter and for the next week I experienced those pangs so achingly familiar to anybody who has ever been in love. One makes allowances. The letter has to get there. Probably one just missed a post and therefore it didn't arrive the following day. So no need to panic. She would have got the letter on the second day ... No, probably she couldn't get out of school to collect it. So allow another day. Now she has it, she has read it, probably two or three times, and is wondering how to reply in kind. My letter must have been a revelation to her, for what young girl could resist such extravagant expressions of adoration? Even if she *replied* that same night she couldn't post it that night. She would have to wait for a suitable opportunity. So don't expect anything yet. No news is good news.

But after six days, no news started to become the unthinkable.

Even so ... there could be other reasons. She could be ill. I wrote again in even more florid prose. I cribbed from Rupert Brooke, because all is fair. I made the excuses for her, I said that she wasn't to worry that I hadn't received a letter in return, because it made no difference to my feelings.

I waited again for a further week. My work suffered. I thought of nothing else. By the end of the second week I had convinced myself that she was dying, or worse still that my letters had been discovered and that her martyrdom at the hands of the nuns was in progress. My ideas of convent life were inexorably bound up in fragmented misconceptions gleaned from the turgid volumes of the lives of saints in Canon Gotto's library. I conjured up a startling vision of my beloved held captive, forced to deny me, doing penance.

Straight away I began to make plans. I obtained a one-inch Ordnance Survey map of the district and planned the route I would take. Porthleven to Newquay proved to be some forty miles. Bright with my one desire, I obtained permission to absent myself on Saturday, carefully checked and oiled my bicycle, and retired early on the Friday evening.

I live as a jaded traveller now. A journey of seven thousand miles is a jumbo-sized chore, a boring race against the clock. The daily fight along the M4 to London, even in the smoothest of limousines, adds another crease to my belly – a mere seventeen miles in an insulated box, and we grow old in the traffic jams, breathing nothing but our own polluted air. The soul is no traveller any more.

That day, that Saturday when I folded and packed my best suit into the holdall on my bike, my spikey hair watered into submission, setting out on such a journey of promise, my legs anxiously spinning the miles away ... that feeling will never come again. Yes, of course the temptation is there – how satisfying to colour yesterday's sketch-book with purple splashes – and yet sitting here at my desk, burning more of my midnight oil, I can without remembered guile pinpoint every turn of the wheel, older but no wiser, setting out once again as a fool, and certain to return so.

I left Porthleven at first light and was through Redruth before ten, pushing the pedals relentlessly, sustained by anticipation of certain joys to come. By a quarter to twelve I stood on the high land overlooking the bay at Newquay. There I went behind a hedge to change my clothes. That accomplished, I cycled slowly into town.

The map fades. I retain nothing of the geography of the streets or houses. I remember that I enquired the location of the convent school. Presumably I dismounted nearby. Did I eat lunch? I have no recollection. I know I waited, but how long I waited ... Was the sun shining? Were there other people in the streets? Faded images. Negatives of snapshots that were never printed. But no suggestion of defeat, that much I do remember. It never occurred to me that I wouldn't glimpse her, that was inconceivable.

There was a sort of happy ending. She did appear, I did see her. At some point during that afternoon a group of school girls snaked out of the courtyard, marshalled by nuns, and Marguerite was amongst them. The projector flickers, the action is jerky, a few frames are missing, but I can discern from this distance in time the progress of that giggling column as it crossed the street to the cliff-top and walked down the steps to the beach. I followed at a distance.

From the top of the cliffs I saw the group arrange themselves on the sand, the nuns black against the virgin beach, sinister blobs in the midst of all the innocence. I had never taken my eyes off Marguerite, watching her as a sniper watches his selected victim.

The rest is banal. Pulp magazine fiction. I went in search of some gift for her. I was blinded with love. I spent all my sweet coupons on a box of chocolates. I returned to the cliff. They were still there below me, but now I saw that Marguerite was sitting apart from the rest, almost as if she sensed my presence.

I walked slowly down to the beach, watching the guardian nuns carefully every inch of the way. Taking a long detour once my shoes felt sand beneath them, I casually worked my way nearer to Marguerite. I dared not give any signal, I could only hope that she would look up and see me approaching.

I was almost alongside her before this happened. Then everything went very swiftly. All I could remember afterwards was that I no longer had the box of chocolates in my hand. I was filled with shame. It could only be that I had dropped it in the sand beside her, a panicky gesture, completely out of character with the suave lover of my preparations, but I could not bring myself to retrace my steps. Useless, drained, I walked on to the harbour and thence up another set of steps to the promenade. When I got back to the beach and looked down she was nowhere to be seen.

It was Tuesday before I received a letter from her. By then I had dispatched three, each one more passionate than the last. Her letter was brief. She thanked me for the chocolates, which she said were scrumptious; she thanked me for taking the trouble to come all that long way, and she signed herself with love.

I was, of course, transported. Alone in my room I went from the writing desk to the mirror over the basin, finishing a page of humbleness and then examining my face in reflection. It seemed scarcely possible that I had not changed. I started to wash with extra care. I felt the need to be perfect for her.

The following Saturday I received my second letter from her. It was a long letter and it returned my love in full. In it she outlined a plan for our next meeting. She was to receive a visit from an elderly cousin who, she assured me, would be sympathetic to our cause. Chaperoned by this adult, she would be allowed to go her own way for the entire day. It was to be perfection.

I was up at an unearthly hour that second Saturday. I completed my toilet with infinite care, arranged and rearranged my best shirt and trousers, saw that my shoes were polished then washed again.

We had arranged to meet a short distance *out* of the town and, when I arrived on the high ground overlooking the long sweep of the bay, everywhere was calm and·a warm and lazy breeze flew in from the sea to dry the morning grass.

She came punctually and her 'elderly' cousin – who proved to be a girl in her late twenties – wandered off after some desultory exchange of pleasantries, doubtless confident that her young charge was in no danger. We were alone, and the summer day stretched limitless before us.

I have no faded snapshots of her, no mementoes, no trace whatsoever, and, although my memory is as vivid as a badly stitched appendix scar, I have no recollections of the actual operation. All I can recall is that she was not wearing her school uniform when she greeted me and that she was the protagonist throughout the hot blur of that day.

We walked to a deserted beach and there, presumably, took some picnic lunch. I can't be sure. I don't remember going into any cafe. I found it difficult to look at her – does that seem possible? We must have talked, we must have held long and involved conversations, so much is certain, and yet nothing remains. You would have thought that everything about that day would have stamped itself indelibly on my mind, but such is not the case. All that love I could so easily confide on paper vanished without a trace. All I can evoke again is that sickening feeling of inadequacy that burned into me more fiercely than the sun, the rising panic I felt as the realisation that I was allowing the precious minutes and hours to slip away without progressing my cause.

She was, I now realise, bored with me, irritated by my passive adoration. I suppose I was totally unprepared at such close proximity for the revelation her superb young body offered. She too had made her plans and she came wearing a flowered bathing costume under her thin summer dress. There, beside me on the beach, she stood and removed the dress, artlessly, casually, then sank again to the sand, turning inwards towards me so that the full lushness of her breasts brushed against my arm.

Nothing in my far from timid imagination had conditioned me for the real thing. That revealed and sunburned flesh so close to my seaward-turning head, that mass of tumbled hair falling to touch the first swell of unkissed breasts had too much reality and I was powerless. With infinite regret I record here that we never exchanged one fumbled kiss – she was chaperoned by my turgid purity that day and perhaps that is why I remember her more vividly than those in whose arms I later lay with fonder delights.

How did I take my farewells? Did I see the cousin again? Were any promises given? Was hope completely extinguished before the afternoon ended? I don't know. I suspect I was even more stupid than these recollections suggest. I began the long journey home, dissecting every incident with each push of the pedals. On one of the steep hills before Redruth I overtook an old woman bent with the weight of her shopping bag. I dismounted and went back to her and offered to carry her parcels. It was a deliberate action, not my good deed for the day. I was challenging God, I dared Him, in the face of my conduct, to shatter my happiness.

He gave me a completely Old Testament answer. A few agonising days after that Saturday afternoon I got a brief note from Marguerite. In it she said that she did not wish to see me again, that she considered it a waste of time to continue our association, and she signed herself, With All Good Wishes, or some such cruelty.

There is a postscript. Two years after the events I have described I achieved a certain local fame by becoming the Question Master of the BBC's Junior Brains Trust. My photograph appeared in the now defunct *Illustrated* and I entertained certain conceits. Armed with these, I went in search of Marguerite. I remembered the town she lived in and went there. I enquired at the local post office and was given an address. It proved to be out of date, but the present tenants furnished me with the new one.

Boldness being my friend, I presented myself at her door. Her welcome, when she had recovered from her surprise, was quite genuine. My fame, such as it was, had apparently preceded me. We walked out together. I met her parents and she was taken back to Newbury Park to meet mine. For a few days we were inseparable, but, as her enthusiasms blossomed, so mine withered. Despite her beauty (for the early promise had been fulfilled) she no longer had the power to destroy me. I kissed her goodbye one evening and I never saw her again. Her letters to me went unanswered, so that all we shared in the end was a common cruelty.

JULIA CARLING

Julia Carling, beauty guru and glamorous TV presenter, writes a regular beauty column for the Daily Mail. She is currently filming a new television series, has co-authored the beauty book Beauty Scoop, *and is also immersed in a four-year diploma course in Egyptology – as well as being a mother of two.*

actually, it's **love**

Big on Love

Personally I'm big on love. I'll take it whatever way it comes: hugs, kisses, gifts, memories, happiness, sadness, all in any package. Love can speak volumes yet you don't have to say a thing.

I probably love too much and cause myself my own heartache if I don't get the same amount back, retreating to a corner feeling sorry for myself. I can, however, guarantee one thing at that point, which is that I will get a wet, black nose snuffling in my ear from my Labrador dog, Biff. Now nine years old, he is one solid lump of bad-breathed love that can cheer me up in a second, and all with just a look.

As a puppy he may have chewed through an entire kitchen table and chairs, dug up a freshly laid garden, plants and all, and peed on my bed and duvet enough times to make me scream. But I'm glad to say all those are now memories of pure love.

When I walk in the door I have children tugging at my ankles all screaming for immediate attention, and then there's one black hound at the back of the queue waiting patiently just to get a pat on the head.

His love is unconditional whatever mood I may be in, and takes on the rest of the family members as part of the job. He doesn't care that my younger daughter pulls on his tail and ears enough to make him wince, or that my elder daughter can't resist a gentle kick in his direction when he's lying on her toys, but just one look towards me for reassurance and he takes it all in his stride.

He is the one being I know who is completely faithful, loyal; however he might be feeling in himself, the love never stops, both towards me and towards all those I love too.

Who could ask for more?

PHILLIP HODSON

Phillip Hodson, one of the UK's most renowned relationship counsellors, is a fellow of the BACP, an eminent psychotherapist and a visiting university lecturer. He is a seasoned broadcaster and author of several bestselling self-help books, including his most recent, Your Perfect Partner.

actually, it's **love**

Mystery of Love

I was once completely besotted with a beautiful girl who had some intriguing, even peculiar ideas about how to conduct a relationship. For instance, she'd give me precise instructions about where we should meet, what time and so on, but I wasn't allowed to speak and had to follow her suggestions. In other words, she took the initiative. She got extremely turned on by this element of mystery, and so did I – at first.

We lived in this fantasy world for some weeks. While it was very arousing, it obviously wasn't a very practical way to carry on. My boss didn't understand that Tuesday was our day of silence.

I also began to see (I was a bit young at the time) that her need for play-acting and mystery came from real difficulties in her personality. I wanted to develop the relationship but she was stuck in her fantasy world.

But I loved it while it lasted.

NIAMH CUSACK

Niamh Cusack is renowned as a classical actress having played three of Shakespeare's major heroines – Juliet, Desdemona and Rosalind – for the RSC, and Portia at the Chichester Festival Theatre. Most recently she appeared in His Dark Materials *at the National Theatre.*

actually, it's love

The Language of Love

Like most people I know, I have done many ridiculous and humiliating things in the pursuit of love and the loved one.

When I was sixteen I had a serious crush on an intense young timpanist in my youth orchestra. D had frightened, gentle, green eyes and a halo of fuzzy hair, and I was his for the asking. After a few passionate discussions on life and music in coffee shops, culminating in nothing more than a chaste peck on the cheek, he invited me to a charismatic prayer meeting. I wasn't sure what this would entail, but it was definitely the date that I had been angling for.

That fateful Sunday morning in my most feminine dress and clogs (do you remember when clogs were fashionable?) I turned up at the address my beau had given me. It was a large family house in a wealthy suburb of Dublin. I was greeted by two smiling, middle-aged women. E had an other-worldly look in her eyes and very clean teeth, while H seemed much more earth-bound and bossy. D was already having coffee (coffee? *Before* the service? We Catholics never got coffee until after we'd done our praying) with some others from the group. He welcomed me with a gentle hand on my arm (he *touched* me!) and introduced me to the others.

After coffee, we were ushered into another room with chairs arranged in a circle. Someone read an excerpt from the Bible and then started to pray. Then another woman read a bit and she too started to pray. Others joined in. The disconcerting thing about these prayers was that they were in a strange, gobbledygook of a language. Sometimes it sounded like Latin and then it would metamorphose into something different. At first I wanted to laugh but, as all around me, including my beloved D, were deeply into the chanting with eyes firmly closed, I realised they didn't see the joke. As the cacophony of muttering, singing and whispering grew, I considered running away out of the room but realised that this would mean losing my heart's desire.

Well, I thought to myself, I'll join in too. I'll pray in Gaelic and nobody will know the difference. So off I went muttering my repertoire of prayers with an ear to the general chorus so that I wouldn't be left on my own with my version. After an hour and a half of crescendo and diminuendo in the religious fervour, the meeting wound down to a peaceful and friendly silence. We then dispersed with fond farewells at the front door.

D took me to the bus. Not a word was spoken of the morning's events and with the usual peck on the cheek he made his escape. We never had another date.

It was only later that I learned how charismatics speak in tongues, the language of the Holy Spirit, a language of no earthly abode, and so only the genuine charismatic can speak it. No doubt D knew what a humbug I had been, and all my romantic dreams were scuppered.

BERNARD COOKSON

Bernard Cookson is the highly regarded cartoonist whose work is regularly to be seen in national newspapers and magazines. As an illustrator he has collaborated on The Lighter Side of Today, The Great Disaster *series and, most recently,* Chelsea Chicks *and* Bloomsbury Babes.

actually, it's **love**

Bear Truths

I think the greatest influence on my life was undoubtedly Rupert Bear.

He was immensely likeable, clever, resourceful and was forever having exciting adventures. Mum and Dad Bear seemed ideal parents – loving, caring and just sufficiently indulgent to allow Rupert enough space to enjoy his escapades with his dear chums Algy, Pug, Bill, Edward and Podgy. Life at the delightfully picturesque cottage in Nutwood seemed idyllic.

The weather always appeared to be perfect, nobody was ever really disagreeable and I am convinced that Rupert's early influence on me was such that I suspect ever since I have been (albeit subconsciously) through love of him trying to arrange my own life along similar lines to that of Rupert and his chums at Nutwood.

GEORGE MELLY

George Melly, a living legend in the world of jazz, is also a writer, critic, art lecturer and voiceover artist. He is also the author of more than a dozen books including Rum, Bum and Concertina *and* Mellymobile.

actually, it's **love**

All That Jazz

In the 1950s I was a singer with a jazz band and travelled about the country in an unreliable van staying at the cheapest digs we were able to find. I had a certain reputation among fans but my life, while lively enough, was by no means luxurious. Then the *Daily Express*, Manchester edition, decided to put on a travelling variety show called Rhythm with the Stars, and not only was the band I sang with part of the bill, I was also booked as compère for the entire venture.

Among the other acts was a glamorous young woman whom I shall call X, then famous as a cabaret artiste and tired businessman's dream. My sex life at that time was varied and full, but it certainly didn't include people like her. I was surprised therefore that during the run of the show she took me under her wing, despite considerable opposition from her manager, a formidable woman who clearly disapproved of our liaison. I was still more surprised when, on the very last night of the show, she invited me into her bed.

The next day we all went our various ways, and to be frank I didn't expect to hear from her again. Then that evening, when we were appearing in a small corn exchange in Norfolk, the manager approached me with an air of suppressed excitement and awe, to tell me that X was on the telephone. X told me that she had to see me again – was desperate to see me again – and was it possible that I could make it up to Sheffield the following week where she was appearing in variety?

Naturally, although I could ill afford it, I went up there at the first opportunity, only to be told by her manager that X had a bad headache and couldn't see me. I returned to London in quite a bad temper, but had no sooner entered my flat than she was on the phone again explaining that she really had had a terrible migraine and could I *please* come to Cardiff on the following Monday. I did, only to be told, yet again, that she must have dinner with her agent and our meeting was impossible.

This time I made up my mind not to listen to her any more, but a long and loving telephone conversation with her, and a promise that this time it would be different and that anyway her next engagement was in Brighton, helped to change my mind.

I went down to Brighton only to find that, this time, yes she would see me and yes she intended to take me out to dinner, but I would not be alone. Three other previous boyfriends had turned up, all equally convinced that this was *the* night.

I had a bit of a go at X's secretary – how it was obviously she who manipulated my love, refused me entry to the dressing room and had now played this last malicious trick. She looked at me sadly. 'You could be blaming the wrong person,' she said.

With the other suitors I made my way to a public house and got to be rather drunk. X did take us out to dinner, although I have little recollection of it, and no idea how I came to wake up on the sofa of a hotel on the front, and was forced, on regaining consciousness, to battle through a gale to the station to catch the first train. I heard no more.

Some years later, however, I mentioned this incident to someone else in the profession and they said X was famous for going to bed with people once and then having them run around all over the country at her invitation only to discover her entirely unavailable.

She is dead now, but I happened to see her (although I didn't recognise her) in a restaurant a while ago. She greeted me. She had grown to be very fat but was extremely friendly, and by this time I couldn't really imagine my anguish some forty years before. At least I've never forgotten her, and realise that what I did for love, while genuine at the time, makes me look a total idiot.

YVONNE ROBERTS

Yvonne Roberts, award-winning newspaper and television journalist, is the bestselling author of Every Woman Deserves An Adventure, The Trouble with Single Women *and* A History of Insects. *Her latest novel is called* Shake.

actually, it's love

Burma Bound

Each week, my cousin Cath, aged eighteen, and I, aged ten years and nine months, were delegated to clean the attic bedroom. Cath's older sisters, Peg and Jeannie, were responsible for the two bedrooms on the first floor while my Aunty Min cleaned the ground floor. This included the front room (kept for best), the sitting room (the size of a caravan lounge, gleaming with brass and china knick-knacks) and 'the back' – the prefab kitchen with a corrugated iron roof which doubled up as the only bathroom and bolt hole for anyone who wanted to smoke an illicit fag.

Muzak for the Sunday-morning clean was provided by the screams of the seagulls in this north Wales seaside town, and the voices in the chapel next door – 'Bread of Heaven! Bread of Heaven ...' – plus *Two-Way Family Favourites* turned up full blast. The posh English voice of Jean Metcalfe would plaster over all the lust and longing with banal messages from outposts of the British Empire. 'Bill in Akrotiti sends all his love to Nancy in Stockport and says it won't be long now before he's home. The message is in the song.'

'Each night I ask the stars up above, why must I be a teenager in love?'

'What's BURMA?' I'd ask Cath as we both lay on the bed while she wrote love letters to Bill, her fee-aan-saay (the more syllables, the more significant the promotion from spinster to about-to-be-spouse).

'It's a place.'

'But Bill's in Yorkshire, not BURMA,' I persisted, a young pioneer in pedantry.

'BURMA is a place you go to when you're older.'

'How far is it from London?'

'Far enough for you not to know about it.'

Cath did a jive around the room with an imaginary partner. *'Chantilly Lace and a pretty face … a wiggle in her walk and a giggle in her talk.'* Cath could wiggle, *really* wiggle. She was born blonde but took to the bottle, bleaching with gusto from the age of sixteen. Now she was almost cream haired. 'Is it natural?' a lad would occasionally ask.

'Natural?' Cath would say. 'Natural? Of course it's not bloody natural. What do you think I am? A bloody Albino?'

Cath always had an answer. A quip, a bit of backchat.

Cath and I were a team. 'Cleaning' the attic was a doddle. Switch on the Hoover, spray a couple of squirts of furniture polish into the air – and lie on the bed for a good

110

forty minutes or so doing nothing. Occasionally Peg or Jeannie would catch us out. Once Cath concussed Peg on the bedhead because Peg said we were lazy cows. Peg lay there pale faced, skinny legged, her net petticoats stiffened with sugar standing to attention. She looked like an overturned standard lamp.

'Christ,' Cath said, laughing, impervious to Peg's condition. 'I'd hate to be the bloody undertaker who lays you out.'

If it had been me who'd knocked Peg out, I would have been worried sick that I'd killed her. Not Cath.

In 1959, in a non-conformist, highly conformist society in which women weren't impregnated by men, they miraculously found themselves 'in the family way' bringing shame and temporary excitement to the entire community; in 1959, a time when everybody cared what everybody else thought about what everybody else was doing, wearing, saying – Cath genuinely didn't give a damn.

'Now, she's a wild one, isn't she?' they'd say to my Aunty Min. And, 'She's got too many brains for her good, that girl.'

I affected to be totally, utterly unimpressed by Cath. She had breasts; I didn't. She had jokes; I didn't. Cath worked in an office; everybody else worked in the washing-machine factory. Cath wore tight, short, white skirts even in winter. She also wore the most up-to-date winkle-pickers, pale blue chunky-knit M&S cardigans with whalebone buttons the size of saucers; and when her hair was done, secured in place by a sticky iron cobweb of hair lacquer (one and sixpence from Woollies) and her pale apricot lipstick had been fixed and checked in the mirror over the fireplace in the lounge, she was a Star.

Every time some pea-brained adult asked me, 'And what do you want to be when you grow up?' I'd usually say – a creep to the last – 'A missionary doctor.' But honestly, what I wanted to be was Cath.

'Fancy coming out on Friday?' Cath asked casually during one of the weekend cleans.

'Out? You mean at night?'

'Yeah. I'll take you for a treat.'

This conversation was difficult a) because I'd grown accustomed to the idea that being 'nearly eleven' barred you from almost any activity that was remotely interesting, and b) I'd caught a glimpse of the inside flap of the most recent envelope dispatched from Bill to Cath. (I was always sent from the room while Cath hid her cache of letters.) BURMA was written across the top and then a word was suspended from each letter like a flypaper from a light bulb.

Be Undressed ...

'Well, do you want to come out?'

Ready My ...

'We'll go to the Blue Lagoon in Llandudno. I'll buy you a milkshake and you can put some money in the jukebox.'

The Blue Lagoon had only been open a few months. It had one of the new cappuccino machines which served two mouthfuls of coffee in Perspex cups; it had stools on spindly legs; and, above all, it had a jukebox. The first jukebox in Llandudno.

Angel ...

'What will Aunty Min say?'

'She won't mind if you're with me. We'll just say we're going out to bingo or something. It'll be smashing. Trust me.'

I always did because, if Cath was there, there was always a good time.

Be Undressed Ready My Angel. The sentence suddenly made sense. Oh my God. I could feel myself go bright pink. BURMA. Be Undressed Ready My Angel. It was a place you go to when you're older all right. It was *rude.*

Cath was packing up the letters, oblivious. 'I'll write and tell Bill that I'm out with you on Friday night. If it's you, he won't mind at all.' Bill and jealousy, like egg and bacon, always went together.

'You take care of her, mind,' Aunty Min shouted from the front door on the Friday as we ran like hell for the bus, laughing fit to bust.

The Blue Lagoon was a fug of smoke. Everybody knew Cath and acted as if I was invisible. I couldn't have been happier.

'I had a girl. Donna was her name. Since she's been gone, I ain't never been the same ...' was being played over and over again, the jukebox whirling and clicking to select the same 45, the whole performance neon-lit like fireworks on Coronation night.

Cath sat at the bar and ordered a cappuccino and a strawberry milkshake. *Then she lit up a fag! In public.* Aunty Min would kill her.

'Want one?' she said, then laughed. 'Only kidding.'

Ten minutes later, Paul arrived. He was tall and slim and had a shock of blond hair just like Cath's – except that I don't think his came out of a bottle. He might have been a real Albino, but I couldn't see if his eyes were pink since he was wearing dark glasses. In February.

'Paul's got something to show me,' Cath said. 'I'll be back in five minutes. Gloria'll look after you, won't you, dell?' Gloria, behind the counter with hoop earrings the size of lifebelts, looked at me suspiciously.

'You wanna something-a?' Gloria asked. I shook my head. I was the only nearly-eleven year old in the whole place. If I sat still long enough, I thought to myself, perhaps people would forget that I was nearly eleven.

After half an hour Cath still hadn't come back. Perhaps this was a test. Cath was testing me out. I was happy. Happy to be invisible. Happy to be in on something – although what, I wasn't quite sure.

According to the clock in the shape of a Coke bottle

top, Cath had been gone for fifty-seven minutes when she suddenly popped up again, fizzing. 'C'mon, kid,' she said. 'Let's get some fish and chips.'

'Where's Paul?' I asked. Cath was struggling to get her engagement ring back on. She gave me a hug as we pushed our way to the door.

'Now listen, kid. Can you keep a secret?'

I nodded.

'If anyone asks you, Aunty Min, Peg, Jeannie, Bill, if anybody asks you, say nothing about the Blue Lagoon. Say nothing about Paul. Don't say a word. Promise?'

'Who is he then?'

'Nobody, he's just a friend.'

'Why can't I say anything then?'

'Because if you do,' Cath said, 'I'll be bloody murdered.'

'Really?'

'Really.'

We came home on the last bus after a night to remember: cod and chips and a trip to the amusement arcade. I'd forgotten that Cath's life lay in my hands. I'd forgotten that if I really loved her – which I did – I'd have to lie. Not lie accidentally, spontaneously which I did all the time. But lie *knowingly*. And who knows how God might react?

'And what time do you call this?' Aunty Min was waiting at the front door. On the table were cups of tea and ham sandwiches to 'tide us over' until the morning. 'So what have you been up to then?' she asked as we sat around the fire. Cath gave me a wink.

'I've been to Burma,' I said. 'With Cath.'

BRUCE OLDFIELD

Bruce Oldfield, OBE, international fashion designer, started life in a Barnardo's home and became designer to the world's most glamorous women. He was the favourite couturier of Diana, Princess of Wales and continues to make both couture and ready-to-wear collections. His earlier designs feature in fashion museums around the world.

actually, it's **love**

Missing the Bus

About twenty-five years ago while at teacher training college in Sheffield, I was due to go on a trip to the London galleries with our art department. I was particularly keen to go because of a hot crush on a fellow student (unrequited to this day). Unfortunately I missed the bus, but I decided that, by hook or by crook, I was going to London if only to sit next to her all the way back in the coach to Sheffield.

I started to hitch-hike down the M1, but luck wasn't with me that day and I finally arrived at the pick-up point in Russell Square to see the coach pulling off the stand.

I never told anyone about this little adventure. I felt, and still feel, extremely stupid. But true love is not meant to run smoothly, and it rarely does.

JO FOLEY

Jo Foley, writer, journalist and former editor of Woman, Options *and the* Observer Magazine, *is now a highly regarded travel writer and author of numerous health and beauty books including the bestselling* Great Spa Escapes.

actually, it's **love**

Journey's End

We stood on the small hillside looking across the flat, fertile plain towards Macroom and beyond into the blue haze that was the county boundary between Cork and Kerry. This is where he wanted to be – buried with his father but looking towards Kerry where he had met my mother and where I had been born.

'Come on,' he said. 'It's going to rain and I want a drink.'

We moved off. I didn't want him to get cold or wet – he didn't have that long to live and if he did die I wanted it to be in bed, in the warmth, not on the rainswept path of a country graveyard. As I looked back at my grandfather's grave, I could not help but smile. Daddy had done it again. Only he would have got me to his own grave with such natural ease plus such a fine sense of the theatrical.

Later, as we sat in one of those old side-of-the-road Irish pubs which smell of turf fires and porter, I opened my second packet of cigarettes of the day. Neither he nor I felt any sense of irony in my behaviour. He was dying of lung cancer and I was at that time smoking sixty a day. As I puffed away and sipped a single glass of Guinness (I was driving), he knocked back the whisky and told stories as he always had, of times long ago, of people long since dead and of incidents that were somewhere between fact and fiction.

He was a wonderful storyteller, always had been, and with his soft lilting voice he could keep people captivated for hours. He also had a prodigious memory and could remember times, places and who said what to whom sixty years ago as if it had only taken place last week. He also knew hundreds of poems and stories and songs off by heart.

One of my earliest and fondest memories is of clambering into bed with my Daddy on Saturday mornings where he would sing to me and tell me stories. Often he would make me cry because the songs and the stories were so sad. So poignant were his renditions that he would cry along. This would enrage my mother who thought it heinous to make a child cry. We loved it.

In between the weepies he taught me a lot of Wordsworth, a little Tennyson, a great deal of Yeats and some really suspect ballads. I must have been one of the few five year olds who was word perfect on 'Upon Westminster Bridge' and 'The Face On The Bar-room Floor'.

So here the two of us were, having a last wander through the places of his life in Cork and Kerry. Even though we knew it was the last visit, it was anything but a sentimental journey. For someone who practically invented sentimentality, my father was not in the least mawkish about his own dying. And that rubbed off on me. I could think about it, talk about it and deal with it.

Nearly eight months later we were sitting together again talking and having a drink. This time I wasn't smoking: I had kicked the habit I had nurtured and loved for nearly a quarter of a century with five hours of aversion therapy. I had gone from three packs a day to zilch after the first session. I had, I thought rather foolishly, promised my father on the day we were told of his cancer, that, if he never smoked again, I would give up at the end of the year. Nothing like shutting the stable door …

As I poured him another drink, he looked at me with his slow, sly smile.

'I never thought you'd give them up,' he said. As I have explained there was nothing sentimental in the approach to his living, so I gave him back my slow, sly smile.

'I never thought I'd have to. I thought you'd be dead and wouldn't hold me to my promise.'

We clinked our glasses and there was very nearly a tear in his eye. He died later that year – at one o'clock in the afternoon on Christmas Day. Such a fine sense of the theatrical, and I've never smoked another cigarette.

SIR CLIFF RICHARD

Sir Cliff Richard, OBE, the UK's greatest hit-maker, has sold over 250 million records in his forty-six-year career: he is vice president of the Christian relief and development agency Tearfund.

actually, it's **love**

A Loving Appeal

That first morning in Bangladesh I must have washed my hands a dozen times. I was there on behalf of the Christian development agency Tearfund, and I made a beeline for every standpipe we passed, furiously washing my hands for fear of catching something.

Everyone in the camps we visited, even the babies, was covered in sores. I was trying to keep everyone at arm's length. Then, as I bent down to one little mite, mainly for the photographer's benefit, someone accidentally trod on the child's fingers. He cried out and, as a reflex, I grabbed hold of him forgetting about the dirt and the sores. I remember now that warm little body clinging to me, and the crying stopped instantly.

A Third World image, previously sanitised and kept at bay by TV bulletins, became reality: a statistic became a person. Through what was to be an appeal for funds, I'd encountered an appeal for love. In that moment I understood how starved these children were of love as well as food. Parents hadn't the strength or the inclination to show it: survival was too exhausting.

I didn't know it at the time, but someone had taken a picture of me, ashen faced, with the little boy buried in my shoulder. Today an enlargement of that snap is one of my most treasured possessions. It hangs on the wall between my bedroom and my bathroom where I cannot fail to see it and remember.

NEIL KINNOCK

*Neil Kinnock, former leader of the Labour Party,
has had a long and distinguished career in
politics and is now vice president of the
European Commission. His books include*
Making Our Way – Investing in Britain's Future
and Thorns and Roses.

actually, it's love

Crossing the Line

She was blonde. She was sparkling. She was an angel. She captured my every thought. And, like me, she was nine.

For days I found excuses to arrive at school at the same time, to leave school at the same time. I grasped every opportunity to fool around outrageously, climb over spiked railings, walk along high, narrow walls. I would tell any story to intrigue her, fight any fight to impress her (I didn't get the chance), take any risk to enthral her.

Still she made no response.

Driven beyond all sane judgement, I showed the ultimate boldness: I crossed the invisible line between the boys' junior school playground and the girls' junior school playground … and held her hand.

It was a dare. It couldn't be resisted by anyone impelled by my passion and my mates' goading.

Of course, I was spotted. The riot of screeching laughter made that inevitable. In any case, what was the point of such reckless gallantry if it wasn't noticed?

This was the flogging fifties before the swinging sixties. Retribution came. A twelve-inch ruler brought down with force, three – or was it four? – times on my right hand. Did they know that it was the hand that once, for a fleeting moment, clasped the divine fingers?

Perhaps not. It did not even seem to bewitch my beloved. I think she became attached to someone else. Anyway, I gave up love for several weeks. And it was a long time before my heart took me across any more invisible lines.

ANNE DE COURCY

Anne de Courcy is the author of 1939: The Last Season, The Viceroy's Daughters, Diana Mosley *and* Society's Queen: The Life of Edith, Marchioness of Londonderry.

actually, it's **love**

The Proposal File

Proposals fall into a number of different categories. There is the Proposal Romantic, the Proposal Cautious, even the Non-proposal (seen in its most classic form in the former Jagger–Jerry alliance). The most dangerous of all, undoubtedly, is the Proposal Reneged-on – and I'm not just thinking of Cecil Parkinson. You may remember the case of the district nurse, jilted by a nearby village doctor, who took details of their four-year affair – including a sheaf of fancy pictures he had taken of her during a Kenya safari – and sent them to the General Medical Council.

'He had cold feet, and he wasn't going to marry me,' she said in this modern substitute for the breach-of-promise case, adding, as she poured out dates, times and the distress it had caused her, 'I don't want to be malicious, just truthful.' What it did for wildlife tours I don't know, but the doctor was suspended for nine months.

Most people remember where they made or received a proposal. Tony Benn proposed to his late wife on a park bench. Clearly not only a romantic politically, he then went on to buy the bench for £30, embellishing it with a plaque to commemorate the event, and installed it in the Benn garden (as a safe seat, one is tempted to say).

My own first proposal came when sitting in the back seat of an aeroplane built for two. As far as categories went, it was a bit of a hybrid. 'Say you'll marry me,' he shouted over his shoulder, pointing the little plane into a terrifying dive (we were above the Isle of Wight at the time). 'Or else ...' As Cowes zoomed up to meet us I realised only one answer was possible.

As keen students of the romantic will already have noticed, this one was a mixture of the Rhett Butler ('Say Yes, Damn You!') school and the Pre-emptive Strike, the whole lightly coated with the flattering implication that life without the loved one is not worth living.

It also contained – though I was too scared at the time to notice – one classic ingredient of the Proposal Passionate: a sensation of total helplessness in the face of another's overwhelming determination, examples of which abound throughout romantic fiction.

There is Jane Eyre, listening transfixed to Mr Rochester: 'You – you strange, almost unearthly thing! – I love you as my own flesh. You, Jane, I must have you for my own – entirely my own. Will you be mine? Say yes, quickly.'

Or Catherine Gaskin, queen of the lending-library shelves, whose hero Lieutenant Andrew Maclay declaims (in *Sara Dane*):

'You've driven me crazy – witch! I don't sleep nights thinking about you. And I keep my watches like a drunken fool. I can tell you it's been hell! Sara, will you promise to marry me and let me have my peace back again?'

In strict contrast is the Proposal Matter-of-Fact, where peace has clearly not gone missing for a single second. Listen to this choice example from Daphne du Maurier's *Rebecca*, whose anonymous heroine hears her wildest dreams come true in words only fractionally more arousing than a British Rail platform announcement.

'So that's settled, isn't it?' he said, going on with his toast and marmalade. 'Instead of being companion to Mrs Van Hopper you become mine, and your duties will be almost exactly the same. I also like new library books, and flowers in the drawing room, and bezique after dinner. And someone to pour out my tea. The only difference is that I don't take Taxol, I prefer Eno's, and you must never let me run out of my particular brand of toothpaste.'

In love, it is often better to travel hopefully than to arrive. Hence the Proposal Cynical, somewhat akin in sentiment to the famous Groucho Marx definition of exclusivity ('I wouldn't want to join the sort of club that would have me as a member'), and here expressed by Ralph Walsh Emerson:

> The accepted and betrothed love has lost the wildest charm of his maiden in her acceptance of him. She was Heaven whilst he pursued her as a star; she cannot be Heaven if she stoops to such a one as he.

A sub-category here is the Near Miss, perhaps the most familiar of all male excuses. 'Marry you?' said Candide. 'Those words have opened my eyes to the imprudence of my conduct. Alas, dear idol of my life, I am not deserving of your goodness. Cunegond is yet living.'

Few of us will be at the receiving end of the Proposal Regal. Here is the eighteen-year-old Queen Victoria describing Albert's acceptance.

> 'We embraced each other over and over again, and he was so kind, so affectionate. Oh! to feel I was, and am, loved by such an Angel as Albert was too great a delight to describe! He is perfection; perfection in every way ...'

Even the Proposal Regal opens with modest flutterings and veiled hints ('I said to Albert I thought he must be aware why I wished him to come here'), but today ritual hesitations are no longer a part of the mating game. Here is Jilly Cooper's version of the Bed and Breakfast Proposal – her heroine, Emily, meets the impossible Rory at a party on Friday evening, goes to bed with him the same night and on Sunday, after a particularly golden moment in their forty-eight-hour relationship, he proposes to her.

> 'I'm bored with living in sin,' he said a couple of hours later. 'Let's get married.'
>
> I looked at him incredulously, reeling from the shock. 'Did you say you wanted to marry me?' I whispered. 'You can't – I mean, what about all those other girls after you? You could marry anyone. Why me?'
>
> 'I'm kinky that way,' he said. 'I'll try anything once.'

As a justification of the two-night stand this glimpse of a busy weekend in Fulham could not be bettered. But back in the days when the Big O was merely one more capital letter, the blinding power of passion was just as apparent. One of the most erotically charged sentences in all literature is, for me, the moment after Elizabeth Bennet has finally accepted Darcy: 'They walked on without knowing in what direction.'

For the true Proposal Romantic contains not only limitless love, with its scent of gardenia petals, its dazzling fountains of desire, but hope, joy, promise and the sense of a wider world. May you never have to ask in vain.

DAVID HAMILTON

David Hamilton, radio and television DJ currently hosting his own daily show on Saga Radio, has, in the last twenty-five years, helped raise over £3 million for charity as a member and president of the Showbiz Eleven football team.

actually, it's **love**

Holiday Romancing

I first fell in love at fifteen while I was on a family caravan holiday in Walton-on-the-Naze. One wet afternoon, I amused myself by driving around on the dodgem cars. Business was very quiet and the only other driver was a very attractive girl at least a year older than me (which seemed a lot then). We literally bumped into each other.

One thing led to another and later that week I discovered the joys of the birds and the bees on the cliff top.

I returned home a lovesick teenager. I lost my appetite and even my interest in football, which normally dominated my every waking moment. After a couple of weeks I arranged to visit my first girlfriend and cycled the long journey from my family home in Wimbledon to hers in Waltham Cross on the other side of London.

Sadly, when I got there I discovered all the magic had gone. The electricity that existed between us on the cliff tops had blown a fuse. At the tender age of fifteen, I learned the terrible truth about holiday romances – they seldom survive the journey home.

WENDY PERRIAM

Wendy Perriam, bestselling novelist whose books include Lying *and* Tread Softly, *also teaches creative writing at Morley College in London. Her recently published second collection of short stories is called* Virgin in the Gym.

Just William

Most of my great love affairs have been, alas, tragically unrequited. I suspect it's my own fault for choosing curs and bastards. But just *one* relationship with a genuine cur and bastard was ecstatically mutual.

It was love at first sight – no doubt about it. As the sickly, trembly scrap of a puppy fixed me with his Bournville eyes, I too went wobbly at the knees, flung myself upon him and covered him with hot wet kisses, instantly reciprocated. We spent an unconventional first night together – he under the bed, me in it – but by dawn he was on top of me; I relished his warm and sensuous weight.

I named him William, after William Rufus, since he was both regal and red – an Irish setter, with an Irish temperament to match – volatile, passionate, neurotic, unreliable, and with those smiling Irish eyes.

I remember our first row. He wolfed a large elaborate birthday cake I had made (and iced) for a ninety-year-old aunt, and later threw it up in my study on the proofs of my latest novel. He also ate my black fishnet tights and, over the years, several dozen toilet rolls – though actually personal hygiene was never his strong point, as he had an incorrigible tendency to roll in things unspeakable.

Fortunately, I was well practised in washing muddy sports kit (my first husband was a rugby fiend), which stood me in good stead when it came to washing canines. The bath tub would end up full of grit and hairs, the bathroom semi-flooded, but oh! how handsome William looked once I'd burnished his coat with henna and bay rum, and spent long hours with the hair dryer.

Sometimes he misunderstood the purpose of all this titivation, assuming it was for the benefit of rival females. And what bitter pangs of jealousy I suffered when he slinked off with some lucky bitch, or spent the night with his current bit of fluff, sidling back next morning with a truly hangdog look. But I hadn't the heart to stay sour when he pressed his nose so passionately into my groin, or left love offerings on my bed: a soggy half-chewed slipper, or the most precious and malodorous of his bones. And anyway I knew, deep down, that I had never been so idolised in any previous relationship. What other male would follow me all round the house, sit on my foot while I worked, and gaze at me adoringly, or greet me at the front door with an impassioned aria of top-C barks and yelps, when I'd only popped out to the postbox?

So when he finally died (an event so tragic it is best passed over in grim black-bordered silence), I knew I had to make some recompense for all he had given me, pour out my appreciation for a lifetime of devotion. His funeral, I decided, would be a genuine labour of love – no expense nor effect spared.

My second husband (a woodwork fiend) set about crafting his coffin – none of your cheap whitewood, but finest grain mahogany, with real brass handles, and lined with a magnificent velvet curtain in Tyrian purple. His shroud was my best Harrods dressing gown – a Chinese silk creation, printed with peacocks, symbol of both love and immortality. We filled his coffin with grave-goods, in the manner of Tutankhamen, to prepare him for the Other Side – a big fat juicy marrowbone, chicken breast in jelly, chocolate Doggy Drops. I composed a funeral ode, an elegy modelled on those of Catullus, with overtones of Shelley's *Adonais*, and agonised about the choice of requiem. Would Verdi's be too theatrical, Fauré's too emotionally intense?

On a dark day in November, the funeral guests assembled in our garden – my parents, our three children, the neighbours from both sides, and assorted friends and relatives. My daughters laid the wreath – red roses, again for love, entwined with evergreens to represent the everlasting vigour of that love. My stepson was in charge of the cassette (we'd settled on the Verdi) and soon the strains of the 'Dies Irae' were thundering over the privet hedge. When I rose to deliver the funeral address, solemnising William's official passing to the Great

Lamppost In The Sky, there was not a dry eye in the house.

The obsequies over, I served tea and Spiller's Shapes (spread liberally with Pedigree Chum), and we talked fondly about the Dear Departed, recalling the high spots of his life: the time he jumped off Teddington Bridge in pursuit of a black swan; his Tuesday-evening Obedience Classes (he restricted obedience thenceforward to Tuesdays, after dusk); the embarrassing occasion when he cocked his leg over the vicar's calf-skin shoe.

Once the guests had departed, my husband crept back to the now moonlit garden to fill in the grave and plant a weeping willow, weeping himself beneath the mournful moon.

A fortnight later, I attended the cremation of a nonagenarian aunt. The coffin looked like chipboard, a vase of plastic lilies stood on the so-called altar, and there was no address or ode – only two wavering low-key hymns accompanied by a bronchitic organ. As I watched the cheapskate coffin glide away behind tatty Dralon curtains in a startling shade of electric blue, I whispered to my husband, there and then, would he please order more mahogany and sharpen up his saw. I had decided to be buried in the garden, not in any soulless crematorium, so that I could be beside my Beloved for all eternity.

RIP.

GEORGE BAKER

George Baker established himself as an actor of note in the 1950s swashbuckler film The Moonraker. *But it was playing the title role in the highly successful TV series* The Wexford Files *that made him a household name. He is currently working on his own scripts.*

actually, it's **love**

This Thing Called Love

What I did for love begs many questions. The greatest of these is 'what is love?'

Love, poor damaged word, is used to persuade the reluctant to respond.

'I love you, don't I?'

'I love you, Gwyneth.'

'Oh, Dai. Here you hold the bible, I'll take them down myself.'

The love of country for which men are prepared to die and take their brothers with them.

The love of air, rain and the forest, which is a joke among men.

Infinite love, an archaic concept, but 'I know that my redeemer liveth ...'

Love, a blessed word full of laughter, understanding and friendship. The foundation on which lasting relationships are built.

I first properly understood the word when I was with my wife and she was dying of cancer; it is a word made up of spirit, courage, joy, acceptance of universal thought and, above all, laughter.

What did I do for love? I watched with wonder. I live to emulate and laugh, because 'love casteth out fear'.

JULIA LANGDON

Julia Langdon, journalist, author, political commentator and the first woman to be appointed a political editor in Fleet Street, contributes regularly to radio, television and national newspapers. Her books include the bestselling biography of Mo Mowlam, and currently she is writing a biography of the Chancellor of the Exchequer, Gordon Brown.

actually, it's **love**

Politically Correct

If all politicians are mad – and no sane person can really have much doubt about that – then anyone who chooses to spend half of the day and most of the night working in the company of loonies must be pretty far gone along the trail. Why do it? Why, for love of course.

For love, for toothpaste and for tomato ketchup. The latter two relate to another sort of love and we'll get to them in a minute. The main point is that one can only stand such a crazy job if one truly has a passion for politics. Otherwise, it would drive you mad.

I rather like it when people ask what I do for a living. 'I hang around in bars,' I reply somewhat smugly. This has the virtue of being true, but is additionally attractive because it is ever so slightly shocking. It's like when the mother-in-law's friends used to ask what I did before I was married. 'Like sleep around, you mean?' I would challenge them, for the hell of it.

Ah, but that was long ago when girls like me weren't expected to 'do anything', let alone hang around in bars.

But that, dear reader, is the lot of the parliamentary lobby correspondent.

You want to know how the government's plans are going down? You go to the bars. You wish to hear the gossip? Then perhaps a few hours in the early evening around the main watering holes. You would like to find out what ministers think is going on? Take them out to lunch or dinner and talk about it over a glass of wine. And as for what is really happening? Well, there's nothing to beat a few drinks after the ten o'clock vote when the atmosphere is usually really pretty relaxed.

The wine virgins among us are quite careful about all this booze, not least in order to remain wise. That means you have to remember what people tell you, otherwise the exercise would have been fairly pointless in the first place. A love of politics involves a relish in relating its intricacies. And it's important, too, to remain sober and keep your wits about you, not only because some inconsiderate proprietor might ask you to put some of this down in print, but there is also the possibility of the midnight emergency.

These come in many forms. Sometimes it's just an unexpected political wriggle that has emerged in the morning blats. Sometimes it's the whisper of the rumour that may bring down a minister, or even a government. Sometimes they telephone you, these barmy politicians, in the early hours of the morning to pour out their hearts about either their policies or their popsies and you hear them out, you let them talk it through.

Out of love, really. Love of politics, because it's never dull and it matters. Love of politicians, because, be they great or small, they are only human. Love of the very humanity of it all.

And because you have to buy toothpaste and tomato ketchup.

'Don't use too much of that!' I shout at those I love. 'Don't you realise I have to go to work to earn the money to buy those things?'

'But you love it,' they say – and they're right.

JOSS ACKLAND

Joss Ackland, CBE, is one of film and theatre's most admired classical actors thanks to a career which has included playing C. S. Lewis in Shadowlands *and opening the Barbican in* 1 Henry IV Parts 1 and 2. *More recently he starred in the award-winning* First and Last. *His films include* White Mischief, Lethal Weapon 2 *and* The Hunt for Red October.

actually, it's love

A Fishy Tale

Much as I disapprove of the Englishman's dispro-portionate love of animals, I suspect somewhere deep down that I too have been affected by this lunacy.

When I was a young boy I was given some fishing tackle as a birthday present. As I was an evacuee in Bedford, I took my new rod and line to the River Ouse where I caught a fish, proudly took it home in a bucket, then placed it in our bath where it swam back and forth.

My mother was furious when she saw it and told me to get rid of it. So I walked all the way back to the river and threw it in. As far as I know it still swims there today.

Over fifty years later my wife and I were staying in Italy when we were plagued by rats and mice. Eventually we put down some poison. One morning I went to have a shower and there were two baby mice obviously punch drunk after tasting a snack provided by Lucretia here. So I put them into a cardboard box, drove out to the wheat fields and deposited them in the hope they would recover.

Maybe by now they have met up with the fish in heaven, bragging about who had the narrowest escape.

KEITH WATERHOUSE

*Keith Waterhouse, CBE, distinguished playwright
and author, has produced a whole range of
work for television, cinema and theatre including
the classic* Billy Liar *and the award-winning*
Jeffrey Bernard is Unwell. *He is also the author
of* Waterhouse at Large, *from which this
extract is taken.*

actually, it's **love**

Head-on Collisions

An American book once published over here, *Teenage Romance or How To Die of Embarrassment*, reminds me how little the basics of young love – not to mention young love-bites – change over the years.

Teenagers may dress differently, dance differently, tattoo their heads and talk a language resembling Iroquois Indian but they still worry about their hands sweating when snogging at the back row of the pictures. They still light the wrong end of the cigarette and realise only after flashing on a winning smile that they have a piece of apple stuck between their two front teeth, and they still hang about in the chemist's then leave without buying anything.

Or so we are told by Delia Ephron who wrote this instructive compendium, which contains two valuable pages on How To Hide A Pimple and another two on How To Worry ('Worry that you have B.O. Worry that everyone hates you. Worry that in a long kiss you have to breathe through your nose and your nose will be stopped up …')

Some worries she doesn't mention. Nothing, not even

the ordeal of Romeo and Juliet, can surely match the anguish of two shy young lovers wandering across a buttercup meadow in the shimmering sunset ... both of them dying to spend a penny.

Then when – on the excuse of having a sudden craving for a bag of crisps – they do re-reach civilisation with its welcome public conveniences (what if they're closed?), they both go into the wrong one by mistake.

Worry is to the under-sixteens as bad feet are to the over-sixties. Girl virgins still worry about being pregnant and boy virgins about being impotent ... and virgins of either sex still confide to the dressing-table mirror, 'I know you can't get it off lavatory seats but I think I'm going to make medical history.'

Lavatories, come to think of it, have always loomed large in teenage nightmares. It is more years ago than most of you have had hot flushes, but I still remember the chest-gnawing embarrassment of coming out of the men's room in the Majestic Ballroom, Leeds, colliding with someone carrying a tray of lemonade and returning to my partner looking as if – well, as if I hadn't made it in time. There was nothing I could bring myself to say, there was nowhere she could bring herself to look, and we never saw one another again.

Beyond bathroom range, there are still traumas enough. There must still be the anxiety of waiting for a date outside the Odeon, knowing perfectly well that it was outside the Odeon where you said you'd meet and having a clear recollection of her/his last words being 'See you outside the Odeon' – but she/he is now a full one and a half minutes late and are you absolutely sure you didn't say the ABC?

Can left-handed boys kissing right-handed girls ever be absolutely sure that they're not going to move their heads the wrong way and get involved in a nasty nose-collision like stags clashing antlers?

Don't teenage girls still wrestle with the eternal and insoluble dilemma that they'll be thought too easy if they do and too hard-to-get if they don't? And don't teenage boys still hope for a disturbance from a park ranger or peeping Tom before they're forced to go further than they know how to?

Then there is the enduring suspicion that she reads out the choicest bits of his love letters to her best friends ... that he told all his mates what happened on the towpath that night and that's why they're all giving her funny looks. There is the fear that the boil on his nose might not have cleared up by six o'clock this evening ... and that the wisps in her comb are a portent that all her hair is going to fall out. There is the ever-present possibility that, though her parents are supposed to be in Majorca, the hotel burned down and they are going to walk through the door and switch the light on any minute ... and that, when she smiled at him after that tender moment, she wasn't smiling at all, she was laughing at him.

Hideous, perspiring, stomach-clutching days. And what wouldn't you give to live through them all again?

MAGGIE GOODMAN

Maggie Goodman, journalist and award-winning magazine editor, created Company *Magazine and was the launch editor of* Hello! *and later* Home and Life. *She is currently the editor of* Icon *Magazine.*

actually, it's **love**

All At Sea

I used to be a normal person. I wore normal clothes, used normal language, spent normal weekends with friends and family and went on normal holidays in cars and hotels. And then I met Mad Boatman.

He had a dinghy and something called a surf boat with a shiny, slippery surface, and he spent weekends pitching these against the elements off the grey Harwich coast. Newly divorced, his excuse was that this was something to keep his teenage boys amused – better than going to the zoo. The boys, however, soon lost interest and I became the recipient of his fanatical desires.

The first time I went in the surf boat, a gust of wind blew me silently off it. But Mad Boatman, manically playing with his sails, didn't even notice until a passing helmsman drew his attention to this pathetic creature almost drowning, certainly not waving.

It was a cold and wet romance built on panic and relief, violent argument and hysterical laughter, sweet nothings inaudible against the wind, physical attractions lost beneath waterproof layers of Michelin Man proportions.

Then everything changed. Mad Boatman decided to build a boat. A big boat. An ocean-going trimaran with cabins and galleys and enough room to take six people round the world. Mad Boatman did have a day job but he assured me this little project could be knocked off in a couple of years of weekends. Small sacrifice, I thought.

It took seven years. Seven years of weekends and holidays in a Thameside shed peopled by fellow maniacs who could have walked straight out of a David Storey play. Mostly I left him to it because on my rare visits to the shed I was overcome with gloom at the amount still to be done. The coast of England is littered with the hulls of half-finished boats, and I was guilty of little faith.

But I stayed around, occasionally enticing Mad Boatman away for a holiday (flotilla sailing in Turkey, what else?) until the great day of the launch in St Katherine Dock. Rashly I promised unlimited champagne for the party, and everyone we'd ever met seemed to have found out.

Thus began stage three of this sea-going love affair. The Mad Boatman could take more holidays than me, so he was forever setting off with fellow mariners and arranging to meet me in far-off harbours. The problem here was his enduring optimism even in the face of the first two laws of the sea: everything takes longer than you imagine, and something always goes wrong.

'Take the ferry to Roscoff and I'll meet you,' he'd say, meaning every word. Or 'I'll definitely be in Gibraltar waiting for you on Friday.'

Fog, calms, storms, fouled propellers – even bad hangovers – inevitably intervened. Bitter experience forced me to set up complicated communication arrangements with bemused third parties; I also insisted on not leaving home until he'd actually arrived at an agreed destination and promised to stay there.

Then there was the cash-flow problem. Whoever invented the phrase about sailing being like standing under a cold shower tearing up five pound notes was seriously misinformed. You can't even get a grommet for five pounds. In its short life, this boat had three engines (yes, it *was* a sailing boat), a new mast, new railings, new sails and every single navigation instrument updated to the state of the art. I couldn't bear to work out the cost, but it had to be more than hiring a luxury yacht to sail round the world.

I was not alone in my love-hate relationship with Mad Boatman and his floating toy. Friends clamoured to join me in being cold, wet, frightened, uncomfortable and shouted at. And they came back for more. As I did.

Sometimes I dreamed of a mellower future where the boat was moored permanently in a picturesque French harbour and made only the occasional foray into the deeps. But this fantasy was shattered fairly early on. 'I'm thinking,' said Mad Boatman one day, 'of doing the transatlantic next year.'

He never did. But if he had, guess who would have been soaking wet, bedraggled, complaining right alongside as he set off? Of course I would. Now, every time I think of Mad Boatman, I think of Mark Twain's words: 'Sail away from the safe harbour. Catch the trade winds in your sails. Explore. Dream. Discover.'

And we did.

PADDY ASHDOWN

Paddy Ashdown – the Right Honourable Lord Ashdown of Norton-sub-Hamdon, KBE – was formerly leader of the Liberal Democrats. He now lives in Bosnia where he is the international community's high representative.

actually, it's **love**

A Military Sin

I was only eighteen when I met my wife Jane. At that time I was in the marines and the rule was you could only get married after the age of twenty-five. I actually quite disgracefully got married ten days before my twenty-first birthday in 'military sin'. We had to ask the permission of the lords of the admiralty in order to do so, and even then it remained difficult. We weren't allowed quarters or marriage allowances and, as my job required me to go abroad a lot, Jane had to make her way to see me by hitching lifts on RAF aircraft around the world.

PAUL NICHOLAS

Paul Nicholas, singer and star of television's Just Good Friends, *was also co-producer of* Grease *and* Saturday Night Fever. *One of the original stars of* Hair, Cats *and* Jesus Christ Superstar, *most recently he starred in a tour of* Fiddler On The Roof.

actually, it's **love**

Stuck on You

I'm tempted to tell you about the time I woke up next to a transvestite – the big feet gave him away – but on second thoughts I'll tell you how I seduced my wife.

I was on tour with the original production of *Hair* and I'd fancied Linzi for weeks, but I was too shy to do anything about it and couldn't pluck up courage to ask her out. Finally, in Manchester, I managed to install myself in the room above hers in the flats we were allocated. One night – it was about two o'clock in the morning, actually – I knocked on her door and asked if I could borrow some glue because some piece of furniture in my room had broken. It must have sounded quite ridiculous, but Linzi, who is an extremely practical person, obviously thought she'd found a kindred spirit. She invited me in and we've been stuck together ever since.

PENNY VINCENZI

Penny Vincenzi, bestselling author of Old Sins *and* Wicked Pleasures, *began her career working for* Vogue *and* Tatler. *She later worked as fashion and beauty editor on several magazines, before becoming a full-time novelist. Her latest book,* Into Temptation, *completed the trilogy* The Spoils of Time.

actually, it's **love**

Tracking Down Love

Romance, one might be forgiven for thinking, is, if not dead, then certainly a bit poorly. In an age when girls dance with girls and boys with boys, when the dinner bill is split between two credit cards, and thanks for a nice evening sent by email, one could well think that a couple would proceed briskly from a handshake to a complete relationship without wasting time on anything soppy in between.

Reader, one would be wrong. Romance is alive and well and setting hearts a-flutter just like it always did. Indeed, I defy any heart out there not to flutter in sympathy with the stories I have to tell you.

Take my friend Francesca, for instance. Married to a film man for more than a year or two, he rang her from Czechoslovakia (they make films in esoteric places these days) very early one morning to hear her sobbing. (You should understand she is not a great one for sobbing in the normal course of events.) She had flu, a temperature of 101; she had a crisis at work and simply had to get in;

next day she had a child due to be de-tonsilised; life was truly tough. She put down the phone, struggled into work and was sitting at her desk at around midday, holding her throbbing head, trying not to sob some more, when her secretary came in and said, 'You've got a visitor.' It was her husband.

Now, before you dry your eyes over that one, try this: a young friend at university was hopelessly in love with someone, and went to a concert with him, and they heard Tchaikovsky's violin concerto together. Very emotional. Next day, still not knowing, she returned to her room and found a record of the concerto placed tenderly under her pillow.

And then there was my friend Angela. A while ago, when living in maidenly bliss in Earl's Court, one morning she found a rose tucked under the windscreen wiper of her car. And the next morning, and the next. Earlier and earlier she got up, and finally she saw him: not a boyfriend, not a smooth city suit, but a workman digging up the road, who had fallen in love with her dizzy prettiness and continued to leave the roses until the road was finally filled in again.

And there was my friend Jackie, who even more of a while ago met a friend in a coffee bar (remember coffee bars?) once a week and, every time they went there, two young men sat and smiled and were obviously much taken by them, but being well brought up apparently pursued the matter no further. And it came to pass that Jackie was invited to a party one night in the wilds of Stanmore or some such, and almost didn't go, but did; and when she got there, standing in the hall clearly waiting for her was one of the young men. 'It worked,' was all he said.

'What?' she asked.

'For the past six months,' he said, 'I have phoned up every single friend and described you to them, hoping that someone would know you. And I have been to every single party I've been invited to because I knew I'd find you at one of them. And I have.'

I liked the rather more simple story of my friend Sarah's boyfriend, who couldn't afford a taxi or even a bus after taking her to the cinema, but spent his last few pence on the evening paper, so she could put it on her head and keep dry from the rain.

My own romantic tale is of a boy (very handsome) I met at the school dance; we waltzed once or twice and then were parted as the clock struck twelve. Thinking I'd never see him again, for we had not exchanged names, and knowing my heart was broken, I was handed a letter a few days later, addressed to 'The Tall Girl In Green With A Yellow Ribbon In Her Hair', which says a lot for my sartorial skills, but never mind. We met and I thought he was awful, but it didn't spoil the romance of the gesture.

Some of the best gestures are quirky, not predictable

at all. Daughter Number Two had a boyfriend with whom words were exchanged late one night. She returned to her flat in tears; an hour or so later the doorbell rang and there he stood, a vodka bottle in hand, the top knocked off to make a vase and a rhododendron flower from the park set inside it. She forgave him everything with no more ado, and so she should have done.

Another friend tells a heart-throbbing story of taking her boyfriend to the airport after he had been staying with her. She drove back home, walked into the bedroom and there on the bed he had prepared a collage of their life together for her: one of his socks, one of hers, one of his T-shirts, one of hers, a tape they had liked, two ticket stubs; any dry eyes out there now?

Of course, the whole point about romance is that you need to like and/or fancy the person proffering it, otherwise it is simply irritating. I can remember feeling nothing but nausea reading a barrage of poetry written to me by a rather intense chap; and a friend whose admirer used to bestow endless bouquets of carnations upon her says, 'He was a pain, and anyway, he knew I didn't like carnations. I just wanted to hit him with them.'

We should perhaps draw a distinction here between romance and love: romance, someone said, is finding a bottle of champagne by the bed, and love is having your side of the bed warmed for you. Romance (said someone else) is having a surprise weekend booked for you, and love is being told about it so you can get your hair done.

Romance is having a weekend away booked for you, and love is your husband sitting you down and telling you that he's cancelled it because he realised you'd much prefer to stay at home and put your feet up.

And love does not have to go in for gestures; it is simply there. The loveliest story I heard was of a wife who decided to sort out her husband's underwear drawer. (Thus does romance lead us.) And right at the bottom of his drawer she found a very old, tattered, office phone directory. And on the back cover were written two series of numbers. Some time later, dabbing streaming eyes, she had realised that one was the phone number of her bachelor-girl flat, and the second was the time of the train he would meet to take her out for their first evening together.

Romance may make the world go round, but love will stop it in its tracks.

SIR RICHARD EYRE

Sir Richard Eyre has won acclaim and numerous awards for his work in both theatre and film. He was director of the National Theatre and has directed, amongst many other films, the highly acclaimed Iris. *He is the author of* Utopia and Other Places *and now divides his time between his twin loves of film and theatre.*

actually, it's **love**

In the Dark

I sit in darkened theatres clutching plastic cups of tea until midnight or fatigue arrive, whichever comes first. I spend good summer daylight hours in windowless rehearsal rooms pacing the floor, talking at length about lust and litigation, judges and jail, vicars and virginity.

I expose my work to critics, some of whom, with the sensitivity of a sledgehammer, point out where I have gone wrong. I've learned the Egyptian national anthem, how to tap dance and the correct way to hold an iguana, all in the name of love.

If love is a kind of madness, then I'm totally insane.

JANE LAPOTAIRE

Jane Lapotaire, actress and writer, is one of the UK's most distinguished actresses having earned a BAFTA for her role as Marie Curie, and starred in London and on Broadway as Edith Piaf in Pam Gems's acclaimed Piaf. *Her third book,* Time Out of Mind, *documents her heroic fight back after a life-threatening illness.*

actually, it's **love**

Tough Love

The human race isn't very lovable – is it?

Children and animals are easy to love – they don't threaten us on the whole. But the shadow side of being human is largely despicable, greedy, vengeful, selfish, warmongering.

Perhaps the most difficult people to love are the mentally ill. I have experienced such love and understanding (often there's no need for words) between people like myself who have been brain damaged and are often truculent, irritable, confrontational and just damned difficult.

But the carers of the brain damaged show the greatest love of all. They help heal wounds that can't be seen, using patience and kindness, often in short supply in the world we live in.

IVAN FALLON

Ivan Fallon, former financial journalist and deputy editor of the Sunday Times, *is now Chief Executive of Independent News and Media (UK). He is also the author of several bestselling biographies including* The Brothers: The Rise and Rise of Saatchi and Saatchi, Billionaire *and* The Player.

actually, it's **love**

Brother Love

Perhaps the most durable and powerful love of my life has been brotherly love. I was born the fifth of sixth brothers, fifteen years separating the youngest, Padraic, from the eldest, Garry. We lived on the south coast of Ireland in a rambling old house within range of rivers, mountains and the sea, all of which we used to the full.

From the moment I could walk, I had to march behind the others as Garry, a self-styled captain in the Fallon Flying Column, led us on day-long tramps up the local mountain, or on expeditions, some of which could take a week by boat up what we pretended were unexplored rivers.

It was Garry too who created the Fallon orchestra which he would solemnly conduct wearing an old pair of tails and using a riding crop as his baton. Beethoven would be on the old record player while the rest of us pretended to play at the appropriate moments on the fake instruments he had made (very skilfully) from cardboard and string. My clarinet was a Moselle wine bottle.

The second eldest, Brian, was the intellectual in what

was a fairly bright family, and would read to us for hours at night. He could recite *Il Penseroso* by heart, although we preferred *The Count of Monte Cristo* and *The Three Musketeers*. From him we learned Edward Lear and chunks of *The Rime of the Ancient Mariner* which I can recite to this day.

When the two eldest left for University in Dublin, the third brother, Conor, took over. He organised fierce games of touch rugby in the winter and test-match cricket in the summer in which we had to be the full current line-up. The 1955 series between England and South Africa was a particularly arduous one for us, playing all day between the cowpats in a glorious summer.

Each of them in his different way was very disciplined in forcing the younger ones to learn properly. We always had guns around the house, but my brothers, rather than my father, set the rules which we younger ones learned – and we respected them.

Niall, the fourth brother, taught us to fish, making Padraic and I practise our casting until our arms ached. Salmon rivers were beyond our reach but we caught brown trout by the creel-load and, in the season fishing off the rocks, some fine sea bass.

Later, while at university, we all continued to be best friends, spending weekends fishing or summer holidays sailing. Marriage and children for all six of us inevitably created other interests and pressures, but never loosened the tight, unspoken relationship between all of us.

In later life, perhaps after the death of both our parents, we made conscious efforts to get together for the big occasions. Garry and Niall both died within two weeks of each other eight years ago, driving the remaining four closer still. As we have grown older, our childhood has assumed an almost mythical feel to it, and the bonds forged then have grown stronger in old age.

ROLF HARRIS

Rolf Harris, OBE, MBE, TV presenter, singer and artist whose work has been exhibited in the National Gallery, is one of the UK's favourite entertainers. Currently he presents the TV shows Star Portraits with Rolf Harris *and the award-winning* Animal Hospital.

actually, it's **love**

Jaded

On a recent tour of Australia I was missing my wife, Alwen, back in England. I felt I had to do something to bring us closer together otherwise I'd go crazy, not seeing her for weeks on end.

So I bought a piece of raw jade and spent the next six weeks carving and polishing it into a pendant. I guess I must have driven the musicians on the tour barmy with the noise because every time they found me I was scraping away with bits of grindstone and setting their teeth on edge.

However, I found it excellent therapy for the pain of separation.

RICHARD E. GRANT

Richard E. Grant, stage, TV and film actor, made his name starring in the iconic Withnail and I. *Since then he has starred in numerous films, including* The Player, The Age of Innocence, *the award-winning* Gosford Park *and* Bright Young Things.

actually, it's **love**

Waiting

'**Y**OUR WIFE IS ON HER WAY TO HOSPITAL BY
AMBULANCE.'

Nine in the morning, last day of filming at Shepperton
and a ghastly sense of déjà vu; we lost our baby daughter
three years before. Born at seven months, she lived for
half an hour. Burying our baby was the saddest of
sorrows.

Again we are at seven months and nausea capsizes
my heart and head. Rush to Queen Charlotte's Hospital
and the waters have mercifully not broken. But blood
spotting. Panic, terror, tears. All-night vigil and Mr Malvern
offers guarded reassurance. 'If your wife does not go into
premature labour, there is a chance. A *chance*. However,
she will have to remain here for the rest of her pregnancy
and move as little as possible.'

The outside world recedes instantly and the inside of
the ward is simultaneously protecting and imprisoning.
Three months bed-bound for Joan. I am contracted to do
another film; I get to the hospital at six in the morning and

leave at eight; I return at seven in the evening until eleven. They waive the visiting-hour restrictions and life has a precarious new routine. This baby means everything. We know she is a girl. We know her name. We see her kick. We tell her to stay inside. Safe.

WAITING. Interrupted by emergency scares and shuffling the trolley up to the labour ward. Not yet. Not now. Hands held together tight. Eyes superglued. All saying. And love so overwhelming, we could bust. As one.

A diet of *Neighbours* and *Going for Gold* with Mr Kelly and *Hello!*; Marks and Sparks is relief from the hospital nosh. Any diversion. However banal. *Prisoner Cell Block H*. Laughing. Holding. Hoping.

Christmas Day and they are both still 'inside'. Kindness and compassion from nurses that we will never forget.

'We can't risk full term. We'll perform a Caesarean section at thirty-six weeks.'

Decision taken and 4 January dated. Four minutes to one in the afternoon and a four-pound, bird-sized baby is briefly 'exhibited' through a glass panel, wrapped tight. Mother still anaesthetised. And water has jetted involuntarily from my eyes like water pistols, and the overwhelming relief has tied my tongue.

One kind of waiting is over, and now I sit beside an unconscious mother-wife and sleeping baby daughter. The relief and silence and profound love is all engulfing.

TIMOTHY SPALL

Timothy Spall OBE, award-winning star of film and television, made his name in Auf Wiedersehen Pet *but has gone on to win acclaim in numerous films including starring in* Secrets and Lies *and, most recently,* The Last Samurai.

Drowned (almost) by Love

Twenty-three years ago I met a girl and fell truly, madly, deeply in love. It was the first time I'd been in love like this and I was very happy indeed.

However, one small problem stood between me and my newfound amour. Three nights a week I was playing the leading role in *The Knights of the Burning Pestle* at the Aldwych Theatre in London, and for the rest of the week I was playing a leading role in a BBC Play for Today being shot on location in the Cotswolds. The problem was that my lover lived in a council flat on the outskirts of Wolverhampton.

Physically I was dividing myself between London and the Cotswolds, while emotionally I only wanted to be in Wolverhampton.

After a couple of disastrous attempts at trying to negotiate my three locations on public transport, I decided there was only one thing to be done – buy a motorcycle. I had been on one before, just often enough to know I shouldn't get on one again, but this was a time for throwing caution to the wind.

So I bought one off an oboe player in the BBC orchestra and, at the first opportunity, loaded the thing on to the last train to Wolverhampton after my performance at the Aldwych. On arrival, I realised I didn't know how to get from the station to my love's council flat, nor how to start the motorbike.

I got it going eventually, and I gave her address to the last cabbie in the station forecourt, saying that I would follow him. My confidence grew by the mile. Soon I was conjuring this vision of yours truly astride a Honda 250cc super-dream American spec job … until the cab shot into a concealed entrance, and I jammed on the brakes bringing me back to reality with a start.

I paid the cabbie and thanked him for his patience. The object of my mission appeared at her kitchen window beckoning me in. I left the machine where it stood and hurried to her boudoir. Within a few minutes, I realised why I had been doing such mad things to get where I was … and the rest is private.

For the next ten days I commuted from Wolverhampton to Cirencester on my trusty steed. My confidence and ability as a biker did indeed grow to the point where I decided to chance the motorway (breaking the law in the process, as I only had a provisional licence). The first two journeys to Cirencester on minor roads seemed to take me via Addis Ababa. By taking the motorway I managed to cut the journey down from three and a quarter hours to just over an hour and a half. This, of course, meant more time with my love.

One morning I left Wolverhampton a bit late (again) and, as I was supposed to be on the Cirencester set at seven in the morning, I had to pretend I was Barry Sheen. The scene to be shot that morning was 'a cricket match in flaming June'. Needless to say it was pouring down.

Anybody who rides a motorbike knows that, without due caution and the correct attire, riding in the rain is no fun at all and potentially dangerous. I was wearing an ankle-length ex-army raincoat done up with one button under the chin, thin cotton trousers and sandals with no socks. On my head I had an open-fronted helmet, old-fashioned goggles (cracked) and wrapped around my face a ladies silk scarf, à la Isadora Duncan, to keep the flies out of my mouth. Nobody was going to take me for Marlon Brando in *The Wild One*. Unlike Isadora, the silk scarf was not about to strangle me, but something every bit as bizarre was about to happen as I hurtled down the M5 at ninety miles per hour, drunk with love and desperate to get my job done on time.

I was OK for time, but by now it was absolutely chucking it down and I was finding it increasingly difficult to breathe. As I gasped for air I seemed to be sucking in water. The more I gasped, the more water I guzzled. I began to panic, feeling faint and almost losing control of the bike. I had enough presence of mind to realise I had to stop.

I pulled on to the hard shoulder where I fell off the bike and into a ditch. When I tried to remove the scarf I found that the G-force from the speed and the water had sealed it tight against my mouth and nose. For a few terrifying moments I really thought I was going to drown.

At last, with one almighty tug, I managed to get it off and breathe again. I could just see the headlines in the next day's papers: YOUNG ACTOR DROWNS ON MOTORBIKE.

By the way, three months later we married.

SIR BEN KINGSLEY

Sir Ben Kingsley, award-winning stage and film actor, shot to fame playing Ghandi *for which he won an Oscar. He has since been nominated three more times for* Bugsy, *and more recently for* Sexy Beast *and* House of Sand and Fog.

actually, it's **love**

(Very) Brief Encounter

What I did for love? I let go.

BRUCE FORSYTH

Bruce Forsyth, OBE, shot to fame hosting the legendary Sunday Night At The London Palladium, *and then* The Generation Game. *He is regarded as the king of variety and TV game shows, and his career has spanned over sixty years.*

actually, it's **love**

The Food of Love

When I first started going out with my wife, Winnie, some twenty-two years ago, I'd always order broccoli whenever we went out for a meal because I knew she loved it. What she didn't know was that I didn't. I like almost every other vegetable, but I can't stand broccoli.

Many years later we were sitting in front of the TV when George Bush came on and declared that he hated broccoli and I blurted out, 'So do I!'

Winnie looked at me and said, 'What do you mean? You love broccoli.'

So I had to tell her the truth. 'I've eaten it all these years because I love you.'

Now I don't have to pretend any more.

JANE REED

Jane Reed, CBE, is the former editor of Woman *and* Woman's Own *and is now a director of* Times Newspapers. *She is also a recipient of the Mark Boxer award for outstanding services to the magazine industry.*

Aunty Betty's Brother

Aunty Betty was one of my widowed mother's group of girlfriends. None of them were 'courting'. Ten years earlier their boyfriends hadn't returned from war; nor had the pool of suitable replacements.

Gwen, Betty, Ruth and Blackie were an exotic bunch in Letchworth, the first and rather socially conscious garden city. My mother was doing 'welfare' at the big hosiery factory in Baldock where Betty was a director's secretary. Ruth ran the village store with her parents at Willian. Blackie was a rare female star in London's rather narrow advertising firmament. She would descend in a cloud of perfume and fur every month or so.

The 'girls' went to the local film club where daring foreign films were shown. They drank gin and its, shopped in the first supermarket and were as sophisticated as you could be in a small, provincial town in the fifties.

Even at ten, I liked Betty's younger brother Tony. He was a lot older than me and my sister, and lived with Betty and their parents in a council house in Baldock. When we went to visit them he was always outside messing about with a motorbike or old banger. He smelled sweaty and his pale hair was greased back.

So when Tony did the most unusual thing of emigrating with them all to Canada, I cared.

Four years later, at fourteen, I was still short, rather chunky, with frizzy hair and freckles. He was long and lean and one day he simply turned up on our doorstep.

He had been to Sweden to buy a Volvo. These were exotic names and concepts. And he was gorgeous – at least to me. He can't have been conventionally good looking because, if he had been, my sister would have got there first. She always did. But he wore a soft, broad-shouldered jacket in big checks of grey and cream. An open neck, pale green shirt, casual slacks, belted. And fancy shoes in two tones of grey with fringed leather golfing flaps. He was bronzed and smiling.

All the males we knew wore scratchy brown tweed and ties.

And he smiled at me. Yes, me. He lifted me from the hot pavement into the seat of this huge car – I seem to remember it as white with red leather, but that could be a fancy – and without another word we purred away from the verge and down to the main road.

That's all it took. My heart was his. I had no thought for myself, how grubby my fingers were, how scratched my legs were, anything. I looked at his profile, and his rather large Adam's apple. I was with this wonderful man. I can feel it now. Almost suffocating with happiness. Did he feel this overwhelming 'thing', too? Actually it never occurred to me to wonder. I was obsessed with this tingling new sensation that was happening to me.

Ten minutes later we were home again, drinking tea, eating Grandma's Victoria cream sandwich cake and listening to his tales of success in Canada. Aunty Betty hadn't done so well, but Tony had made it big. Heaven knows what in, but when they were talking about him later I saw Aunty Ruth tap the side of her nose and lower her eyebrows knowingly.

Tony was due to leave the next day. I think he stayed overnight but such was my innocence I didn't even fantasise about what possibilities that could lead to. I was sure neither my sister nor my mother had the first idea that I was smitten, even when Tony got up early and started to wash the famous car and I ran back and forth with buckets and wash-leathers, breathless as he leaned over me to reach a windscreen wiper. Let me do that, like this … sigh.

My sister had been angling for a ride around the shopping centre in the car since the previous day. She always got her way with men, so I knew she would ruin the last few hours of Tony's stay with us. Three years older than me, she'd introduce him to her girlfriends in town, they'd drink beer and she'd seduce him and, and …

I sat in my bedroom and cried. The misery was exquisite. A small heart breaking for the first time. Hearing my sobs, she came in and asked what the matter was. 'Nothing,' I said. 'Go away.'

She went off and poking my head over the rim of my window I saw her talking to Tony beside the car.

My mother called up that Tony was about to leave. I stomped down the stairs, creased and tearstained. He'd got sunglasses on now. Black ones unlike anything we'd seen in Letchworth. He whipped them off and said, 'Oi, curly. C'mon. I've got half an hour. Let's make the wheels hot …'

I nearly died. I looked at my sister. She was smiling and nodding: go on. I saw her smile at Tony. My mother did, too. Indulgently, affectionately. So they all knew. I didn't care. Didn't feel stupid. I ran and fetched a headscarf and we just left everyone standing there.

I have no recollection of that half hour. Happiness is like that. Just a pink veil of love and joy. We must have talked, we must have returned, he must have left. I no doubt moped around for a day or two … term started. I forget.

But you don't really, do you. You never forget the first time it happens …

ANGELA NEUSTATTER

*Angela Neustatter, journalist and writer,
contributes regularly to the* Guardian, *the* Times,
the Observer *and other papers and magazines.
Her highly regarded books include* Hyenas in
Petticoats, This is Our Time: The Challenge of
Mid-life, *and, more recently,* Locked In: Locked
Out. *She is editor of* Young Minds *magazine.*

actually, it's **love**

Sons and Mothers

My eldest son Zek, then twenty-three, and I faced each other across the restaurant table. His face and voice were full of fury. I'd invited him to eat with me, his brother and his dad, and then suggested he pay for his starter. The way I'd seen it, nobody else was having a starter and so it was fair if he wanted something extra that he use his own money. In his view, not only had I invited him for a meal then made it a conditional invitation – something I would certainly not have done with another adult – but I was also diminishing him, treating him like a child who needed to be taught the value of things.

Earlier this year I sent a brief thank-you note to a friend who, at my twenty-one-year-old son Cato's request, had helped him. I thanked him for being good to my son, saying how grateful I was. Cato was angry. 'It was nothing to do with you,' he stormed. 'Of course I thanked him myself. It's the same as when you want to come to the doctor with me, phone me up at university to see if I'm eating all right, tell me that twenty-one isn't really very grown up when you want me to do things your way. I know I've a lot to learn but you could credit me with some knowledge and social skills, some ability to run my own life.'

These family incidents led me to see that I needed to rethink the way I was as a parent with my sons now that both had passed their twenty-first birthdays and crossed the Rubicon into young adulthood. As parents, most of us assume once we have got through adolescence with our young we can, in the words of a father of two teenage daughters, 'sink into a chair with our feet up'. Not so. It may be difficult for us to recognise them as autonomous beings but that is how they are determined to see themselves, and, if we want a good relationship with them as they move on through adulthood, the onus is on us to rethink and reshape the way we are as parents. Looking back on the family 'snapshots' quoted here, I could see clearly how my actions were an attempt to keep some influence and control over my boys; how, although I didn't acknowledge it, I feared no longer holding sway as Mother Hen. Margot Waddell, consultant child psychotherapist in the adolescent department at the Tavistock Clinic, describes the profound ambivalence for both children and parents:

> It's a time of loss and expectations. There
> can be very real pleasure in watching a child
> with whom you have spent earlier years

building a strong and loving relationship move into maturity, but at the same time there is the sadness at what must now be left behind. It is there in the earliest prototype of the parent who bursts into tears when their child first walks.

In her splendid book *Inside Lives* (Duckworth) Waddell says, 'the way things are negotiated depends on how far parents can bear to relinquish their children. The pain often carries with it intensity and poignancy which tests the bravest of hearts.'

This is hardly surprising if parents have spent the past two decades shaping their lives around children who fill physical time, emotional space and for many of us simply make sense of being there. There can be feelings of rejection as they choose to spend less and less time with us. Elizabeth Matthews, divorced mother of Sophie, twenty-one, feels this keenly.

Sophie and I have always been very close and she has lived with me in the country, quite isolated, so there have been a lot of evenings together like intimate friends. Now we are buying a house together in London and she has insisted we have separate parts with different front doors. I know I can't expect to be part of her social set with her friends and I am aware I must stand back and let her spread her wings. It feels scary.

Wiltshire-based psychologist David Cowell says:

What is needed at this time is a cognitive shift with parents thinking about how important it was for them to gain independence in their time. Sometimes things like playing sports, doing adult activities together, going out for meals and conversation can be a good way of re-forming a relationship so that it becomes more a friendship of the kind you would have with a peer.

Waddell agrees:

If parents can think of the kind of mutually respectful friendships they have with other adults, it provides a good model for how to be with children at this stage. An adult exchange of views is a good thing whereas probably telling them they look tired and should go to bed early is not.

If we reshape the relationship rather than simply cut our young loose, it can be comforting for them. For however cocksure their manner, they often have anxieties and fears at what independence will mean. Zek, now twenty-six, voiced this. 'It's like a film you can rewind. At every point in your life parents are linked to your development, and so it can feel hard to escape their influence and decide who and what you are.'

But parents who make too many explicit and implicit demands, or display disappointment if their young turn against parental values and goals, risk driving their young away. On the other side it can be tough on young adults if parents impose guilt, letting children know how painful their growing up and independent decisions are. Says Cowell, 'Telling kids you miss having them around is one thing, saying you'll slit your throat if they go to New Zealand another.'

London-based child therapist, Louisa Howland, has seen how parents make demands on grown children's time with too-frequent telephone calls, upset if they don't come for Sunday lunch, letting it be known they will be sad holidaying alone if not included in their young's plans.

Parents of young adults have talked to me about how pleasant it can be when they've let go enough to accept their young's help. It may be with practical matters like computers or, as happened with me recently, when Cato stepped in when I was having a difficult time with a work colleague and was becoming absurdly upset. He got on the phone to this person, 'had a chat' and got things straightened out. He told me afterwards, 'I don't want people treating my mum like that.'

There may be particular difficulties for parents who see children preparing to go to university or leave home and realise how little they have known them during the growing years. I interviewed several men and some women like this for my book *This Is Our Time: The Challenge of Mid-life* (Legends Press), hearing deep regret and seeing tears. But however sad this may be it is still possible at this stage to work at building an adult relationship which can be given time it has not had so far to develop.

Parents at this stage can be a valued port of call, offering guidance and help if our young ask for it, rather than trying to impose it. Ben, twenty-two, expressed a common view: 'I wanted the chance to make my own mistakes without my parents saying we've been there, done that, listen to us and avoid coming a cropper. If parents let you make mistakes and are easy about it, you feel able to go to them for advice.'

My sons say the opinionated, discursive, argumentative family life they grew up with where everything was talked about makes it easier to bring problems to us. And although we cannot and should not try to dictate how our growing young should live, Waddell explains, 'Parents sometimes worry about upsetting young adult children by being confrontational but even at this stage children need to know parents have a clear view of how things should be even if they oppose it.'

This is something Barbara Matthews, widowed mother of two sons and a daughter, all in their twenties, feels she had to learn. She says:

> I always took the 'don't interfere' line because I felt it wasn't right to criticise as they were trying to become independent. I now think that, rather than keeping quiet when one dropped out of university and began living a life that was clearly disastrously wrong for her, and when another got into debt, I should have said what I thought. Not speaking honestly was giving up my integrity and in the end that's what children of any age need from a parent.

All in all, once you cut the umbilical cord and take the pressure off by getting a new life, there is real pleasure in watching one's grown kids' adult trajectory. But beware slipping into moments of unguarded sentimentality. Last time I gazed fondly at the boys, murmuring about 'fruits of my womb' in front of friends, they swore if it happened again they would have nothing to do with me again. Ever.

CAROLE STONE

Carole Stone, writer and broadcaster, was for ten years the highly successful producer of BBC Radio 4's Any Questions?. *Now a media consultant, bringing people together to discuss issues of mutual interest, she is also a trustee of the Wallace Collection, and the author of* Networking: The Art Of Making Friends.

actually, it's **love**

My Mother Said

I've lost a lot of boyfriends in the name of love. There was the 'mad Major' who insisted that his dog – a particularly ugly pit bull terrier type of hound – slept in the same bed with us. I should have booted him out – the man, that is. There was the punting fanatic whose life revolved around the Henley Regatta, and for whom I ate too many garlic-laden picnics from the boot of his car, despite the fact that I have an allergy to garlic. Silly me. And then came (or was he before?) the ex-Royal Navy man who made the best RBG – rich brown gravy – in the world, but who puffed on his pipe every waking moment and surrounded us in smoke. Why didn't I point out that he could be seriously damaging our health?

And then there is the one I managed to keep, my husband, Richard: I love him more than all the others put together, but to please him I had to sit through endless Ingmar Bergman films (we nearly parted when I told him *Wild Strawberries* didn't make sense) and feign a devotion to Handel's 'Semele'. Still, he does read the classics to me in bed each night – first time round for me – and it's a joy to fall asleep to the sound of his voice.

But before all these, there was my mother, to whom I was devoted. What have I done in the name of love for her? I try to live my life the way she did. She had a tough time – we were hard up, and my brother Roger suffered from paranoid schizophrenia – but she really did make the most of what life threw at her, changing what she could and accepting what she couldn't. Mama had a huge heart, and an insatiable interest in everyone and everything around her. She let me know how much she loved me, but she never lived her life through me. I can hear her calm voice now: 'Don't worry, darling, it's not that important.' And of course it never was. She taught me to carry on life's journey. Always ready for something new, she took life as she found it – not in little steps but great big strides. Her name was Kathleen. At her funeral I said I would keep alight the flame of her wisdom and her courage. And for the sake of the love I have for her, that's what I'm trying to do.

FERN BRITTON

Fern Britton is one of Britain's favourite television presenters, currently on our screens as a regular co-host of ITV's award-winning flagship daytime show This Morning. *She is equally well known for her role as the presenter of BBC2's top-rated* Ready Steady Cook.

actually, it's **love**

Tea in Bed

Love is everything we say and do. I am very sentimental and it's the small things in life that fill my heart with love and joy. Being brought a cup of tea in bed. Having my hair washed in the bath by my husband. Hiding notes in the children's lunch boxes. The love and care shown by midwives as they do their daily work. The dinner ladies who cuddle away tears at playtime. Costumes made at the eleventh hour year on year before a school play.

Finding the dishwasher has been emptied, the milk bottles put out. Your car is filled with petrol ... and washed. Giving your partner and children the time and space to do the things they want to do. Birthday cakes. Holding hands. Watching *Coronation Street* together. Getting home to find supper cooked, children bathed and ready for bed. Listening to all his stories knowing he will listen to yours. Hearing a child read.

Laughing together. Crying together. Mowing the grass. Eating ice cream. Letting him watch sport. Him letting you watch an old movie. Christmas, anniversaries and holidays. Swimming together in the sea. Bathing the kids, looking through your photo albums together. The way you look at each other. Watching him work when he doesn't know you're watching. The hugs after a row. Standing up for each other. Sleeping in his T-shirt when he's away.

Changing nappies, mopping up sick, remembering to phone. Homemade Mother's Day cards. Cleaning the sink after a shave, putting the loo seat down. Trying not to tidy up all his newspapers and bits and pieces that he likes to spread around.

And waking up together.

RICHARD BARBER

Richard Barber, former editor of Woman, TV Times *and* OK!, *is now a celebrity interviewer for a wide range of glossy magazines as well as being a regular contributor to radio.*

actually, it's **love**

Celebrity Love

The faintly ludicrous way I earn my living is by interviewing celebrities – actors, authors, singers – for newspapers and magazines. They are, by turn, funny, dull, fascinating, self-obsessed and, very often, very rich.

They are also different from you and me because they are famous, and seductive; corrupting fame imposes its own unique pressures. But, as any London cabbie will tell you, we all come into and go out of the world the same way which is very nearly true and something of which I try to remind myself when a particular celebrity is being particularly difficult.

Take the famous in love. Success and wealth may dictate they play the game a little differently but, in the end, love is the great leveller. Helen Mirren is a case in point. The woman once dubbed (to her extreme embarrassment) the Sex Queen of the Royal Shakespeare Company had few rivals in her generation of gifted stage actresses. She has since enjoyed considerable success playing the uncompromising Jane Tennison in Granada

Television's *Prime Suspect*. But, at bedrock, she is a theatre actress, the explanation, surely, for her being made a Dame of the British Empire.

Yet we met in Los Angeles – not a town noted for its strong theatrical tradition – because that is where she lives. And no, she isn't there because she is assiduously pursuing an international film career (though she's appeared in a fair few). The fiercely independent Helen Mirren is there because of love.

The lucky man is her American director husband Taylor (*An Officer and a Gentleman*) Hackford, and the moment she met him, she says, her fate was sealed. 'It's funny, isn't it, but sometimes you do end up getting what you want. I was ready for Taylor. I'd dedicated my whole life up until that point to my work. Anyone who came along fitted in – or didn't. Work came first.'

Dilemma. 'I'm aware,' she says, 'that I mustn't lose my position in the world of British theatre. You've got to be in it to win it, so to speak. You've got to be seen. You've got to do the important work. You can't just dip in and out.

'It's the most terrible tug. If I were to do the sustained body of work I should do, to remind people in Britain I am primarily a theatre actress, that could have an impact on my relationship with Taylor. I've turned down any number of jobs because they would have meant our being apart too long.'

Helen Mirren would no doubt envy the solution of rock

singer Jon Bon Jovi who has just the two women in his life – his wife, Dorothea, and their daughter, Stevie Rose. (The couple also have two sons, Jesse and Jacob.) 'I can rock with the best of them,' says Jon. 'But I sure am happy with these two women. Every man should be as lucky as I am.'

And every man, he says, should do what he's doing: taking his wife to work with him. Fine. But this deep-seated contentment with marriage and fatherhood is scarcely the stuff of hard-drinking, loose-living rock stardom. Jon Bon Jovi is having none of it. 'That's stereotyping,' he says. 'That's judging the book by its cover. I don't hide the fact I have a wife and kids. Actually, I'm pretty proud of them. And, if you look around – from Bono to Bruce to whoever – they're all married, they've all got kids. You can't live your life on television or on vinyl. You've got to be able to enjoy the real things away from the spotlight.'

It's a problem Michael Caine never thought he'd have to encounter. The idea, he says now, that he might one day become an actor was as foreign to him as the notion you could train at an academy for the dramatic arts. Indeed, the only reason he presented himself one day in his mid-teens at a youth club in south-east London's Walworth Road was a girl called Amy Hood. 'I didn't enrol for the drama class,' says Caine, 'because I wanted to act. I enrolled because I had a terrible teenage crush. I knew that in some scenes of most plays someone got to kiss the girl. Unfortunately, Amy was always the lead and I only ever got small parts. So you could say I became an actor to kiss a beautiful girl but failed in my ambition – and look where it got me.'

The rest, as they say, is history, including a long and famously faithful marriage in an industry where silver-wedding ceremonies are not exactly thick on the ground.

Barbra Streisand's romantic history has been altogether more rocky. Her famously tempestuous marriage to actor Elliott Gould (it produced her only son, Jason) gave way to a succession of affairs, none of which led to another trip down the aisle. In the mid-nineties, she fell into the habit of consulting an astrologer. 'I kept being told that I was going to get married the next year. I thought, What do you mean? I haven't been married in years and years. And I haven't met anyone I've wanted to marry. But the astrologer turned out to be right.'

She met actor James Brolin in 1996 when she was mixing the music for *The Mirror Has Two Faces*, the film she directed and in which she starred alongside Jeff Bridges and Lauren Bacall.

'That movie,' says Barbra, 'was a deliberate attempt to break the pattern of all those others – *The Way We Were*, *Funny Girl*, *Funny Lady*, *The Prince of Tides* – in which I never got the man. Well, you know what they say? Fake it till you make it. And, as it turned out, that movie was almost a rehearsal for life. Because it's true: life *can* imitate art. Something, deep in my psyche, I truly believed. But who'd ever have thought it?'

Brolin started coming to watch Barbra at work in the studio. 'He loved the whole experience and kept bringing me cups of tea. And that's how the relationship bloomed. So the film laid the groundwork for my life. Now I feel that, in some strange way, my getting married again came out of playing the woman in the movie who got the guy.'

And yes, she says, love *is* lovelier the second time it calls. 'I know because, from the time I first met Jim, my life has been all about discovering the joy of finding love again, a real bonus at that stage, at that age.'

People who need people are indeed the luckiest people in the world.

ALAN TITCHMARSH

Alan Titchmarsh, MBE, is the UK's favourite gardener. Presenting Gardener's World *and* Ground Force *also established him as a highly regarded radio and TV presenter. He has written more than thirty gardening books, as well as four novels. The Garden Writers' Guild has twice named Alan Gardening Writer of the Year.*

actually, it's **love**

Going for Gold

The first time I fell in love I would lie awake at night wondering if the object of my adulation – the local chemist's daughter – would ever whisper three little words in my ear. She did, eventually, but they were not the ones I had in mind. 'You disgusting thing!' There was an echo about them. It was probably the water in my ears – that and the lofty roof of the swimming baths.

Every Friday night I went there to the Grammar Baths, attached to the school up Cowpasture Road in Ilkley. Hardly Olympic sized, the indoor pool was fifty feet long and twenty-five feet wide, but it had a shallow end where I could just get my nose above the water, and a deep end that I had just proved I could not stand up in. The daft thing was that I could still feel embarrassed even though I'd nearly drowned. Pathetic really, but then I did have a tremendous crush on her.

She was dark and slim, and eleven years old. Her lips and cheeks were pink, her eyebrows neat and black, her eyelashes and sleek bob of hair darkened by the water. I can see her now as I saw her then, clear as day in her green swimsuit. Not that she'd ever looked twice at me except to sneer. Now here I was, lying on the cold wet concrete surround of the pool, shivering and sodden, holding her hand and struggling for breath.

I'd thought quite a lot about holding that hand, but I'd never thought about drowning.

She pulled me out of the pool after I'd gone under three times. I finally decided that, although I might draw attention to myself, waving would be marginally less embarrassing than drowning. I slithered on to the pool surround like a lump of wet cod. Having fished me out and delivered her opinion, she reclaimed her hand and that was it: my first and last physical contact with the object of my dreams, over in a matter of seconds. I was not exactly a hunk at eleven and a half, nor exactly fanciable either, spluttering and panting, trying to rid my lungs of the burning sensation of water. But I did wish she hadn't found me disgusting, even if she had saved my life.

I don't remember seeing her again. We just grew apart. Well, she did. I met her mum a year or two ago and plucked up the courage to ask about her. She'd moved to Canada and become a tax inspector. I stayed here and became a gardener, but ever since then I've wondered idly if my interest in the subject was kindled by the fact that her name was Heather.

ROSEMARY CONLEY

Rosemary Conley, CBE, is the UK's most successful diet and fitness expert. With twenty-four bestselling books to her credit, including The Complete Hip and Thigh Diet which sold two million copies worldwide, she has now sold over five million books. Her online slimming club was launched in 2003.

actually, it's **love**

A Special Friend

Mike, my husband, and I had moved in to rent the west wing of a beautiful country house while we concluded the sale of our new home in Leicestershire in 1996. Nikki, our German Shepherd, plus her daughter, Sheba, moved in with us. Nikki was thirteen years old (a great age for a GSD) and loved life. As Mike and I walked in the beautiful grounds of the house one evening, Nikki saw a rabbit. She ran after it as though she was a two year old. We both looked at each other and agreed that, if she now had a heart attack, at least she would have been enjoying her last moments.

Next morning I went downstairs to make our early morning tea. Nikki was staggering. She couldn't walk. She looked terrible. She spent the day at the vet's. In the afternoon, we had a phone call from the vet to say Nikki was extremely ill having had a heart attack, and that wasn't all. They discovered that she also had advanced breast cancer. The vet explained that it would be kindest to put her to sleep.

I called Mike who said he wanted to say goodbye to her first and, as I was coming home from London that afternoon, we decided to meet up at the vet's to say our farewells to a pet who had been much more to us than just a dog. Mike and I had met at around the time I had got Nikki as a pup. I was living alone at the time and, after having burglars at my office, I decided to get myself a guard dog. Nikki was the first German Shepherd I had ever owned and it seemed quite funny that my new guard dog was a tiny bundle of pup that was seven weeks old. As my work sometimes takes me away from home, I needed a dogsitter, and my new boyfriend, Mike, gladly accepted the challenge.

Right from the very beginning, Nikki played a big part in our flourishing relationship and she went everywhere with us. We loved her dearly and would miss her beyond belief.

We arrived at the vet to be greeted by an exuberant Nikki. Squealing in delight at seeing us, if she could have spoken there was no doubt she was saying, 'I'm fine. Honestly, I'm OK. Please take me home.' We talked to the vet who could see how much better she felt. He told us that, clinically, she was a very, very sick dog but, having seen how happy she was to see us, he agreed for us to take her home.

We knew that her time with us was at a premium but we will always be grateful for that opportunity. We were able to show Nikki how very much we loved her and how much we had appreciated what she had given us throughout her life with us. As it turned out, we had four weeks to love her to bits before she lost her battle for life on 1 May 1996.

LOWRI TURNER

Lowri Turner, TV presenter and journalist, was the highly regarded fashion editor of the London Evening Standard *before she fronted her own TV shows* Lowri, Looking Good *and* Shopping City. *Her first novel,* Stripped Bare, *was nominated for the 2004 WHSmith debut novel award.*

actually, it's **love**

A Labour of Love

The question I have answered all my life is 'What's it like being a twin?' The answer is I have no idea because I've never not been one. It's like asking someone who has never climbed anything steeper than their own staircase how they felt scaling the north face of Annapurna, or enquiring of someone financially challenged what it's like being as rich as Croesus, leaving them wondering which bit of 'irate bank manager' and 'overdraft' you didn't quite get.

I don't mind being asked. It comes with the territory. To be accurate, and to add to the confusion, I have two older brothers and I am actually one of triplets, but Nerys our older sister, was not – as Catrin and I were – one half of the same egg. For all sorts of reasons, Catrin has just always been there. My twin.

Now, don't let's run away with ourselves. 'Always there' is not a mandatory phrase to be twinned – if you get my drift – with 'as one with each other'; she was just physically there. Sorry to be the one to disabuse those who think that twins think alike, dress alike, fancy the same blokes, know when the other is in trouble – not unless it's a phone call or one of us has freaked out right in front of the other's eyes, they don't – twins do not live in each other's pockets, nor do they necessarily want to.

As children we confused everyone else, but not each other. Teachers would have to stare hard to make sure they'd got the one they wanted to tick off or praise. We defended each other as stoutly as we were quick to point the finger when blame was being hunted down. We were separated at school because they said it would be 'good for us' and we couldn't think what they were talking about. When we played, we fought to be the doctor rather than the patient – 'Now don't move until I say so or your arm will fall off' – but would instinctively break a chocolate bar in two to share it.

I don't recall being concerned by seeming to do everything with her. I remember we would squash into the same chair, and we shared a bedroom. Because Nerys had learning difficulties and went away to boarding school, by the time Catrin and I were eleven or twelve we were used to being dispatched to stay with relatives for holidays and we were, out of necessity, dependent on each other to travel alone together.

Physically there are differences, but you'd have to be us or our parents to know instantly what they are. I admit I have, on occasion, walked up to mirrors and said hello;

and I can, and do, confuse childhood pictures of myself and Catrin. The only clue to our identity is often the colour we are wearing. Still, if you look closely, she has a longer nose, a slimmer face and one ear sticking out. She has also grown up to be half an inch taller.

And then we were grown up. Catrin became a lawyer and I became a journalist and eventually a TV presenter, and we met and lived with other people and slid seamlessly into this other, grown-up life. But grown-up stuff brings with it all kinds of issues that make some other, indefinable feeling kick in when the going gets tough. It's an inescapable part of being one half of me and Catrin. Now how can I explain? OK. Try this.

When a year or two ago my relationship broke down and I was left with a two-year-old child and an advanced pregnancy to deal with, it was to Catrin that I turned, instinctively and with an unshakeable confidence that she was my rescue route. It was Catrin who didn't pause for a heartbeat to let me and my two year old move in to her house; Catrin who instantly realised that the house she shared with her partner, Klaus, was more suitable for me and my son while I waited for my baby to be born and that the basement would be OK for them until I could sort myself out.

And it was Catrin who was my birth partner when my baby was born, and Catrin who, not having any children of her own at the time and not knowing what to expect, stayed with me and held my hand when the going got tough.

And then it was my turn to be there for her. But that took a few more months and some shocks for Catrin in how much my life had, and had to, change. I could no longer just get up and go out to dinner, stay awake when I didn't have to, just sit and gossip. Not for a while anyway. And most of all, I remember when the baby was about two weeks old and I was lying exhausted on the bed, having been up half the night and with a toddler to take care of, she came bouncing in to show me a pregnancy test.

'Is it positive?' she asked. 'It is, isn't it? Look. What do you think?'

And I was too tired to do anything more than glance wearily at it and say it was and then collapse back to sleep. The energy to be excited for her, to be pleased for her, was just not there. But a few months later, all that changed.

Klaus, Catrin's partner – and someone I get along with really well – just didn't want to face the whole delivery thing, so I became Catrin's birth partner as she had for me. She didn't have to ask, it was just how it was going to be. Klaus stayed with her until the real business began and then I took over while he sat right outside in the visitors' bit waiting for bulletins from me. And so I held Catrin's hand as she'd held mine, and I grimaced and yelled with her at all the right moments, and told her she was doing just great, made her breathe and mopped her brow, and when the baby was born I held him. I held him first and in the whole of my life I have never felt so privileged.

Now we live just around the corner from each other. Me and my kids in one house, Catrin, Klaus and their baby in another and, no, it doesn't seem odd at all that even now the first person I turn to is Catrin and the first person she turns to is me. Twins, you see. Odd lot.

KACEY AINSWORTH

Kacey Ainsworth, one of the best-known faces in TV soaps, has also appeared in A Touch of Frost, Peak Practice *and Mike Leigh's Oscar-nominated film* Topsy-Turvey. *Most recently she has played Little Mo in* EastEnders, *for which she has won four best television actress awards.*

actually, it's **love**

Cold Feet

I never had a pet of my own except, aged seven, when my sister and I managed to persuade my mother (amid solemn promises of responsibility for their welfare) to purchase a pair of black mice, Sooty and Sweep. As I remember we cleaned and played with them religiously for about three weeks, then my sister or I (I shall say it was her) left the cage door ajar and Sooty and Sweep were liberated.

So at the ripe old age of thirty-three, amid more promises of responsibility for proper training, to my partner this time, I find myself driving to pick up my new chocolate-brown cocker spaniel.

We stand in the kitchen awaiting her arrival, and in scurries a jet-black ball of energy munching a sock. 'She's the wrong colour,' says my partner immediately. The breeder nods and heads off to bring in another puppy. It was then my partner clocked me lying on the floor of a stranger's kitchen in my Joseph trousers being licked to death by the crazy sock-muncher.

'I think we'll keep this one,' he says with a smile.

Fourteen months later, and barely a pair of socks between us, my love for the sock-muncher knows no bounds. We have responsibility for each other. We will go through the years together paw in hand – even if it means getting cold feet.

JULIE BURCHILL

Julie Burchill, newspaper columnist and author of five bestselling books, famously began her career as a 'hip young gunslinger' for the New Musical Express. *Currently she is a columnist for* The Times, *but this extract is her last column for the* Guardian *where, for five years, she was a controversial but a must-read commentator.*

actually, it's **love**

Sayonara, Baby

I woke up this morning and had one lovely brief moment of unconsciousness and then – BAM! – I realised I had to write this column. I turned on the radio and it was the No Doubt cover of that old 1980s song, 'It's My Life' – 'Funny how I found myself in love with you ...' Of course, that started the waterworks going, which woke up my boyfriend.

'What's wrong, baby?'

'I've got to do my last *Guardian* column today, and I'm really, really upset!' He thought about it. 'Well, maybe if it doesn't work out with *The Times*, they'll have you back.'

'That is not an option, you insensitive bastard! And it's not the point!' And I howled louder than ever, as Sting and Craig David singing 'Rise And Fall' came on. The indignity, of crying at Sting and Craig David!

I've never, ever cried about leaving a job before; it's always been school's out! and glee and the-drinks-are-on-me. I've never cried when I got the push, which admittedly happened only the once. I didn't cry when I left free-booting, smash-and-grab papers that would have appeared to be far more natural homes for me and, at the risk of being vulgar, paid far better for my services. I've never even been up to the *Guardian* offices or met the people I worked for! I'd chosen to go. So why was I taking on so?

It was, I think, because, like it says in the song, against all odds I ended up falling in love with the very paper I and my nasty-sexy-greedy 1980s hack friends were most likely to laugh at and least likely to read. When I was first offered a job here five years ago, I was as on my uppers as someone who sits by a pool drinking blue cocktails all day can be. I was Sunny Afternoon and Sunset Boulevard; I, who had written my own ticket since the age of 17, was now in my late 30s and reeling from being sacked by the *Sunday Express*, if you please! Then came the *Guardian*. I had never exactly toed the party line on the Tory papers I'd worked for in the 1980s – I was a fanatical backer of the Soviets in Afghanistan, which made me very unpopular but, looking back, was extremely wise of me; and I believe to this day that the trade unions are the only true defenders of the ordinary man or woman against incipient barbarism. But what we did have in common was a dislike of soppy, sloppy liberalism, the idea that there are no moral absolutes.

When I started at the *Guardian*, though, I couldn't think of anything we saw eye to eye on, except feminism, and even this would soon be arguable as *Guardian* writers queued up to drool over Eminem. They were pro-Irish Republican – I was pro-Protestant. Liberal over crime and punishment – I believed in public hanging. Pro-immigration – I find current levels of white immigration, from democratic eastern European countries, unfair to the immigrant communities already here and harmful to the working class in general in that they drive down the price of labour. Nevertheless, I found myself repeatedly surprised and even humbled by the support and patience the *Guardian* extended to me, this crude cuckoo in the nest, when I kept looking for trouble and finding it.

When I started my *Guardian* column, bitchy mates still in the pay of aforementioned newspapers would sarcastically remind me not to make jokes in it, as my pearls would surely fall on stony ground; because they care about stuff, there was for a long time a perception of *Guardian* readers as, in the words of one posh friend, 'not an awful lot of fun at a house party'. But this hasn't been my experience at all. Though there has been the usual carping, joyless geek chorus, appearing to get an almost parasexual thrill from being outraged by me, I have received thousands of letters and emails from readers displaying such wit and wisdom that I've thought, I wish they were my friend, and, if that makes me seem sad, frankly I don't give a damn.

They were the people who turned what could have

been a me-me-me monologue into a much more lively nudge-wink dialogue; the perfect ear I was pitching for, the unseen mouth I could sense reluctantly smiling, even while they tutted and remarked across the breakfast table that it was about time I grew up. You were the ones – and you know who you are – who stopped it being work and made it fun.

The most common complaint has been, 'But you're so good when you're serious, and write about real issues – why do you let yourself down with all the trivia about sex and pop?' My answer to this would be that to find things like sex and pop trivial speaks unintentionally hilarious volumes about the accuser while saying very little about me. One of my heroes, the architect Clough Williams-Ellis, said of the numerous criticisms of his flamboyant style, 'I would rather be vulgar than boring – especially to myself,' and that just about sums it up.

But five years is five years. And, as I leave, I would refer you back to something I said in my first *Guardian* column of January 1998. 'Hell, I know I've said some evil things about *Guardian* readers in my time, but it's false consciousness and all that. Trust me – I know we can make it.' And we did, didn't we? It's true – this is going to hurt me more than it's going to hurt you: sayonara, baby!

JOHN BIRD

John Bird, MBE, famed for his championing of the homeless, spent his early life in a reformatory where he learned to paint and which led to him winning a place at Chelsea Art School. He launched The Big Issue *in 1991. His critically acclaimed autobiography* Some Luck *was published in 2003.*

actually, it's **love**

The Love Issue

'od chose my toes, he also chose my nose, I chose
G my clothes and most of my blows.'

I wrote this line many years ago when I was sixteen years of age. At the time I was in love. I was in a reformatory for very bad boys – arsonists, thieves and aggressors – and was surrounded by a kind of madness. But amongst it all I had this deep love for Jesus.

What I loved about Jesus was his kindliness to children. His love of fallen women. His dedication to those who were rejected and discarded. That he had more time for the downtrodden than the well heeled.

Jesus was the greatest inspiration in my early life to stop hurting other people and hurting myself. To stop fighting my family and the people who wanted more from me than pain and suffering.

Jesus shines like a beacon above life, a guide for love and an aid to generosity.

Now I am no longer under the spell of the religion that has grown up around him. But I am still glad and inspired by the beauty that he brought into my life when others only wanted to wreak havoc about my head.

Jesus, by his example, delivered the concept of love to a starving child.

ALAN BLEASDALE

Alan Bleasdale, the acclaimed playwright, includes among his many successes Boys From The Black Stuff, *the award-winning* GBH *and* Jake.

actually, it's love

God and Monica Haygarth

Fifty years ago, in 1954 when I was eight years old, I lost my faith in God and replaced Him immediately with Monica Haygarth.

It was an easy choice. For a start, God was *never* there when I needed him, and Monica Haygarth sat next but one to me in class. Visiting priests told us regularly that God was everywhere, but I had never seen him. I couldn't reach out and touch God, whereas I could quite easily reach out across the fat girl who sat between us and touch Monica. Although I think she might have hit me if I had.

Furthermore, God had done absolutely nothing for me. Ever. I had prayed and prayed that my Nanna would get better and she promptly died; I had asked God on numerous occasions to help me beat Peter Whitehead in the sports-day sprint, and every year for three years I had come second; it was also becoming obvious to me that prayer was little use in getting Liverpool Football Club out of the Second Division and, conclusively, however hard I prayed and however hard I tried, I still hadn't learned how to ride a two-wheeler bike. God may have had a hand in my learning to swim, but I suspect the hands that really counted belonged to some older lads who pushed me into the deep end at Knotty Ash baths one Saturday morning.

Actually, upon reflection, I think God had a lucky escape. Even He, renowned in some quarters for His Almighty patience, would surely have aimed a sizeable thunderbolt in my direction if I'd pursued and adored Him in the love-sick manner that I was to pursue and adore Monica Haygarth from 1955 to 1963. Over all those years Monica wasn't, to be perfectly frank, a very good God to me but, God knows, I can hardly blame her.

I don't know why I picked her out for worship. I now remember her to be bright, shy, dark haired, pretty but slightly sharp featured in repose. It might have been that, to my delight, Monica wouldn't let Billy Passmore walk with her on the way to and from school, and I hated Billy Passmore. Not only could he ride a bike, he also had blonde Brylcreemed hair and a huge collection of imported American comics that he would only ever let you borrow if money was involved.

Whatever the reason for my choice of veneration, I cannot think of one Godlike action that Monica performed that converted me; no miracle with the warm school milk, no fancy tricks with the fish fingers and loaves; her wooden desk never did weep salt tears; she did not lay her hands upon my maths book so that I suddenly knew my twelve times table.

Monica Haygarth simply became my God, and there were times when I invested my life in her and her greater glory. She became the constant subject of my bewildering daydreams – or daydream, because there was only one; separate showings but the same film. I am in a trench like I imagined my father to have been in during the Second World War. However, this is a religious war, and there is heavy fighting among the battalions of under-elevens. Every child in my school, St Aloysius Roman Catholic School, has advanced from our assembly hall, through the playground, over the road and into the park. We are behind the railings in Jubilee Park, facing the Protestant troops trapped in Park View School. They refuse to surrender but there is no escape. The school meals van cannot get through and they are slowly starving to death. And damnation. I am a captain, the leader of the infant and junior troops, the brightest boy in the school. I wear a captain's moustache and uniform and a brave smile. Monica and all the girls from St Aloysius are behind the front lines in tents on the bowling green, nursing the wounded and cooking in the captured park-keeper's hut. At night, there is no fighting. It is agreed by both sides. At night, my Catholic troops would retire to the wooden dressing rooms once used before the war by footballers in the park at the weekend. And there, in the dip by the bowling green and the shrubs and the sycamore trees, I would sleep in a big double bed. With Monica. For comfort, comfort alone. I was only eight.

And then I was nine, and then I was ten and then I was eleven. And both my God and I passed the eleven plus. Our grammar schools were fifteen miles apart, but, unlike my first fractured relationship with the God who gave me Ash Wednesday and screaming fears of mortality, never answered my prayers or made a live appearance, absence made my heart grow even fonder for Monica.

This hopeless parading puppy love for Monica was, without her ever knowing, of some benefit to me. Rejection and side effects. For a start, she made me extremely fit, because I had to run at a wild gallop two miles a day, Monday to Friday, forty weeks of the year, to get from where my school bus dropped me off to where I knew she would be getting off her bus and turning around the corner to Page Moss shops. Sadly, when I got there, all I could do was catch my breath and pretend to saunter past her with a warm smile, a nonchalant wave and a falsetto 'Hi, hello'. This was because I lived in the opposite direction to her, and also, let's face facts, because for many years she wouldn't let me walk with her. And that included walking slightly behind or in front of her. And I really was too much of a gentle boy to do anything she didn't want me to do. Well, I might do it until she told me not to do it and then I would never do it again.

Monica was also my fundamental reason for finally learning how to ride a bike. Once I could ride a bike, and my parents had saved up to buy me one, I could then ride it up and down outside her house until it went dark. Or until her father came out of the house and chased me. I must say though that Monica's mother, her grandmother and her younger sister were much more gentle in their approach. They merely laughed at me. Then, one night, Monica came out and told me not to ride up and down outside her house any more. I tried to sell the bike the next day to a lad called McGillivery, but my mother got upset and words like 'HP payments' and 'come here while I kill you' came into the conversation.

However, Monica's greatest unknowing triumph was her massive contribution to my tennis skills. This most reluctant of Goddesses made me by far the best bet for Wimbledon in our parish, for one simple reason: the tennis courts in Jubilee Park overlooked Monica Haygarth's house.

The only pain she ever inflicted upon me, other than the continual pain of polite rejection, was the sacred suffering I had to go through every Sunday morning. For Monica was a very devout and serious churchgoer and she always went to eight o'clock Mass. So to see her on the seventh day, and I had to see her, I worshipped for several years at the altar of my false God, taking Communion and feeling unfaithful to the God two pews in front of me and slightly to the side so I could see something of her in profile.

And on and on and on my pathetic suffering and sad vigil and utter devotion continued. I kept diaries during some of those years. I don't know which I'm more ashamed of now – the near illiteracy or the spaniel I see upon the pages.

10 January 1960. Full Moon. Got 40 lines in Maths. Got into trouble at dinner. Had a fight with Peter O'Gorman. It was his fault. Dinner was pork and jam roly poly. Liverpool's game against United all ticket. Prices gone up. Ground two and sixpence. Saw Monica, but she was very stuck up today. I don't understand. She was very nice yesterday. Bacon, sausage and egg for tea. And peaches.

1 March 1960. Princess Margaret to get married. Cottage pie and semolina. (Ugh.) Didn't see Monica, saw her sister, her sister says she's got chicken pox. Sent her a get well card. Didn't mention not getting a Valentine card. It rained. Had lamb chops and chips for tea.

17 March 1961. Bonney [the headmaster] won't let me drop physics and chemistry, the flaming bum! If it's the last thing I do, I'll get him for it. Mince for dinner with spotted dick. Scored two goals in games. Waited for Monica. She never got off bus. Waited for next three buses. Then went home. St Patrick's Day. When Irish eyes are smiling. I only want one pair of eyes to smile at me. Sausages and mash for tea.

When writing fiction I'm usually careful not to set any dreadful events in April, because I know the temptation to trot out 'April is the cruellest month' would be too easy. However, the April of 1961 lived up to all of T. S. Eliot's expectations. For written large in red ink in my diary on Friday 7 April is the following:

OH BOY! OH BOY! MY RED LETTER DAY! MONICA HAYGARTH SAID SHE WOULD GO OUT WITH ME. ONE OF THE HAPPIEST DAYS OF MY LIFE! AFTER SEVEN YEARS. (I HOPE!!!) THE HAPPIEST DAYS OF MY LIFE: (1) WINNING SCHOLARSHIP. (2) THE DAY WE BEAT THE COLLEGIATE 3–0 AFTER LOSING THE FIRST MATCH 15–1. (3) BEATING LIVERPOOL BOYS 3–2 AND I

SCORED A GOAL AND HIT THE BAR. (4)
TODAY. PLEASE. PLEASE. PLEASE.

9 April 1961. Went to 8 o'clock Mass WITH
Monica! Said she would definitely go out with
me soon. Said she would let me know. Was
very nice. I told her a joke and then had to
explain it. Played tennis for four hours until
nobody else would play. Didn't see Monica.

19 April 1961. One of these days I'll
understand Monica Haygarth. Nearly two
weeks ago she said she would go out with
me, and then she avoids me! Top Of The Hit
Parade is 'You're Driving Me Crazy'. And you
are, Monica, you are!

23 April 1961. Went to eight o'clock Mass.
Monica wasn't there. Her friend Christine
was there. Ended up talking to her for over
two hours. Monica told her to tell me that
she had made a mistake and didn't want to
go out with me and she was very sorry.
Christine was very good about it, said she
understands how I must feel. But she can't.
Went home and stayed in my bedroom all
day. Played Elvis's 'Now And Then There's A

Fool Such As I' over and over again. Didn't have my tea. Told Mum I was sick.

Almost every 31 December for nine years: 'Monica's birthday. Hope she got my card. Will next year be my lucky year?!?!'

1963 was my 'lucky' year. I had, thankfully, stopped writing a daily diary by then, but one of the few entries, for Thursday, 2 May, reads, 'Unbelievably, Monica Haygarth said "yes" – and said she means it this time. Going to see The Beatles, Gerry and the Pacemakers and Roy Orbison on the 26th of May.'

I couldn't – or wouldn't – confess it at the time, not even to my diary, but I have long since faced up to the reality that, firstly, tickets to see the Beatles in Liverpool in the spring of 1963 were as rare as jobs would become twenty years later and, secondly, Monica was a Beatles fan. Get the picture? Uh-huh. But I didn't. I only had the sound turned up.

We went to see the Beatles. We went to see *Laurence of Arabia* and *West Side Story*. One evening I accidentally touched her right breast with my left elbow. Another night we had an argument about God. It was strange arguing about God with someone who had been my God for all those years, for how could I say that I didn't believe in God when I had believed in her for over half my life?

What was much more natural was the terrible shock

upon realising that my She-God was a real person with all real people's strengths and weaknesses, delights and frailties. She must have always known that I was a seriously diffident boy with a weakness for genuflection. But I was stunned to find, when I finally looked, that she didn't quite have the raving beauty of Sophia Loren, the sex appeal of Marilyn Monroe, the singing voice of Dusty Springfield and the wit of Lucille Ball.

We went out with each other for three weeks and then, at the end of one of our increasingly difficult meetings, I never said I would see her again, and she never asked. I stopped going to church and joined a tennis club. I haven't had a God to look up to ever since

Many years later, in the mid-seventies, Monica and I met briefly when we were both schoolteachers and married with three children. She was delightful. Witty and warm and far from shy. And she didn't go to church any more. I was terribly ashamed that I had, over such a long period, pestered her with my ridiculous attentions. I could only think of the misery it must have been to be her and to see me coming.

To my relief and surprise she said that she had, from the very onset, been thrilled by my dedication and glorification; that seeing me half in hiding and waiting was often the highlight of her day. To be adored, even by me, made her feel so special that on many occasions she would wait for me. Before ignoring me all the way home.

I wish that was the happy ending.

But it isn't.

The year immediately after *The Boys From The Black Stuff* was screened was the worst year of my life; like something out of a cheap and ludicrous melodrama. My mother had died suddenly, my father had to have major surgery, both my wife's stepfather and her uncle, two good and decent men, died inexorably and painfully of cancer, her sister-in-law was killed in a car crash, and then, almost unbelievably, our eldest boy became very seriously ill. I think I went out of my mind in 1983, and, if I didn't, I certainly went out to the off-licence. Walking around town, I could see people looking at me and thinking, Oh lucky man, while, inside, I was screaming.

And, as I was saying about cheap melodrama, the very morning that we were to bury my wife's stepfather, the phone rang in our hallway. The front door was open. The funeral cars were waiting in the driveway. I picked the phone up. It was Monica. She was in hospital. She had leukaemia. She wanted to see me.

I never went. I sent flowers. I talked to her on the phone. But I never went. And then she died.

I could defend my lack of action at the time. My defence lay in the paragraphs above and, after all, I told myself, I had only seen her for a matter of hours in two decades. People I knew better and loved more were dying all around me, and our son was blacking out up to sixty times a day. Every day. I just didn't think then that I could possibly take any more grief.

Now, however, despite the passing of the proverbial and the calmness that distance brings, I've been known to come to the unforgiving conclusion that it was the cruellest thing I have ever done to anyone.

Our Monica, who art in Heaven …